Re-Created for Faith

for Faith

TRAINING IN SPIRITUAL WARFARE THROUGH
A MOTHER'S HEAVENLY ASSIGNMENT

ASHLEY K. ADAMS

"Have faith in God," Jesus answered.

"Truly I tell you, if anyone says to this mountain,
'Go, throw yourself into the sea,'
and does not doubt in their heart
but believes that what they say will happen,
it will be done for them.

Therefore I tell you, whatever you ask for in prayer,
believe that you have received it,
and it will be yours."

MARK 11:22–24 NIV

CONTENTS

ACKNOWLEDGMENTS

GOD, MY FATHER,

I would be submerged in darkness without your strong voice of wisdom and direction, speaking to the deepest parts of who I am. You are the Author of life and time, as I am not guaranteed another day. I celebrate each as a gift from above. Thank You, Lord, for your continued miracles here on earth and in my life. Thank You for the most precious gift, full of purpose, my son Carston. We give You the utmost praise, His creator, His redeemer, and His sustainer. Now, God, I ask that you guide every reader with an open heart and mind, reveal Your mysterious ways and ability to make a difference within their situation. Allow them to receive and proclaim Your power in their own lives through my testimony.

All the glory is for you God, in Jesus' Name, Amen.

NATIONWIDE CHILDREN'S HOSPITAL, COLUMBUS, OHIO,

My son's home away from home, for which we will be forever grateful. Thank you to every doctor and NICU nurse who not only helped my son survive but live out every day with as much comfort and elite treatment possible. Whose medical knowledge is much greater than mine, yet respected my spiritual beliefs and requests over my son's life. Due to that freedom, we witnessed many miracles from heaven and souls saved by Christ.

I will never forget Carston's primary nurse, Laila, who hands-down went above and beyond what I could have ever expected for my son.

LAILA,

You loved my son and solely cared for him as if he were yours. Even on the most frustrating days, you bestowed the strongest protection yet most gentle touch. The passion you carry of working with your mind and heart is noticed by everyone. You took the time to study what Carston enjoyed and what he hated; you knew what he needed without the single sound of an alarm. I never had to worry when he was in your care. You were the best nurse for him, and I truly believe God sent us you. When I think of Carston and his life story, I'm always thinking of you.

Thank you.

JUSTIN,

What doesn't break us only makes us stronger together. We have been made resilient and unified as parents. We are deeper in love and appreciation for each other than we've ever been. Through our journey, you continued to financially support us, working long days on the construction site, then treading into the hospital all muddy to sit at Carston's bedside.

Bringing me dinner and a smile, you listened to our day and helped me make tough decisions moving forward. You were there for every crucial moment and continued taking care of things at home and life as usual when life was so hard. You are an important part of me, the solid rock of our family. I know we can get through anything now.

I love you so much.

OUR PARENTS AND IMMEDIATE FAMILY MEMBERS,

I can't begin to express how much I treasure each one of you. From the emergency phone calls, long drives, and hospital stays you endured to the early mornings and late nights watching Trinity, you made it possible for Justin and me to spend all the time we could loving and taking care of our son.

You all helped hold our family together, each in your own special way, and we will never forget it.

⟋⟍

PASTOR TIM AND KIM TEAGUE, PASTOR AARON AND ABBY BEGLEY, AND VICTORY HILL CHURCH,

I stand amazed at the support given through each one of you and our church community. You extended your hand to pick us up through every obstacle during Carston's hospital stay and even after. I will always remember the every Monday hospital visits from you, Pastor Tim, and the special visits in our home and at the hospital from Pastor Aaron. You both went beyond a pastoral position and made yourselves like family to us.

I want to further thank our whole congregation for every prayer, each financial blessing, and the many cards sent in the mail. They uplifted us in our darkest times.

⟋⟍

AMBER DENNIS,

You are so dear to me, my birthing doula and unwavering friend. I love how you so willingly accepted the call of Christ to become my support system through Carston's birth and every day of his life. Not only have you helped educate me in the medical world, but you also lifted my spirit with God's Word and encouraged my trust in the Lord on several occasions. Whenever we were faced with the most terrible news, you were there to recall all the good Christ has done.

I will always remember your place in this journey, right beside me on Carston's couch.

⟋⟍

TUESDAE KING,

We have been together from day one. Of course, we are family, but ever since I can remember, we've been best friends. You know me better than anyone and are always there for a listening ear. You're never afraid to tell me the truth or build me up in times of discouragement. What would I do without my life coach and personal assistant helping me keep it all together? You've played a larger role than you think in getting me through this.

I can only hope to be as loyal and strong for you as you have been for me.

CAROL AND GARY KRASNOUSKY AND
THE CHEERS CHALET STAFF,

Thank you for the wonderful years of memories working with you and your company. The benefit you held in Carson's honor still has me speechless, wondering why so many people would donate their time, money, and energy to support our family. I am so grateful to every employee who chose to give of themselves. You have provided not only a workplace for me but a second family.

You will always hold a special place in my heart.

FOR CARSTON

Y THOUGHTS OF YOU ARE ONES OF PURE JOY AND LOVE. My son, you are the reason for me writing this book. You are my push into a deeper faith; you gave me a greater purpose in this world simply by mothering you and sharing your story. God has chosen you to show His working hand of many healings, peace, direction, and hope. You brought our Lord glory and became a light in the midst of many people's darkness.

Carston, holding you, I always had a warm feeling of joy and peace, humbled that God gave me another day with you because there were many times we were told it was the end. My favorite thing was to rock you in the recliner and listen to worship music. I loved holding you on my chest, so close for lots of warm snuggles. I know music therapy and bath time came second for you, besides cuddling with dad and sister. There were so many precious times we shared, not to mention miraculous moments where there was no medical way...but God made a way.

If in the five months of hospital living, brings one single person to faith in Christ, I want you to know I'd endure it all again. All the times I missed you like crazy, and when I had to watch you hurt, I'm so sorry for that. Having to drive two hours a day to see you. Getting startled throughout the night with calls from your doctor when you weren't feeling well to the point on normal nights when I just couldn't sleep. The days where I spent the majority of my time away from Trinity as she wondered why mommy was always with brother. The times when money was tight and I had to call eight different billing offices to get an extension, calls to SSI, Medicaid, BCMH, and other help;

it was all worth it. You are worth it. Although times were rough, Christ shined through you; He was the light inside you.

Through only your infancy, you have done more on this earth than many of us ever will, the power of prayer was revealed, and all glory was given to God. You're known to be an inspiration, a fighter, an overcomer, a Christ-follower, and leader of many; a miracle, Captain America, and a little ball player always throwing the doctors curveballs! You're my precious son and so precious to many. Every time I see your face, you continue to touch my heart in that special way only you can. You will forever be loved and celebrated, my beautiful Carston. This book is for you.

I love you deeply, Mom.

"I have become a sign to many;
you are my strong refuge.

My mouth is filled with your praise,
declaring your splendor all day long."

PSALM 71:7–8

Carston Ford Adams

A NOTE FROM THE AUTHOR

⟪⟫

THIS JOURNEY IS FAITH IN ACTION. It's not only a story of miracles and physical healing, but how to battle the enemy, trusting in the Lord through all circumstances. The Lord God is the Author of all life, and He created each one of us for a purpose to expand His kingdom in our own uniquely called way. It's not about qualifications or status; God uses people who hear Him and actively move on it. Obedience in accomplishing the small things God has burning on your heart is the key to release an even greater assignment from above. In the midst of our efforts to complete His will, He provides everything we need. He heals, delivers, and restores.

It takes work to follow God deeper, wherever He is leading you, because our hearts must be ready to endure the challenges that come right along with the blessings. We live here in a fallen world with a common enemy, Satan, a spiritual ruler who is very much alive and at war all around us with a very opposite spiritual force than God's. Our enemy wants nothing more than to steal, kill, and destroy us from the inside out. He preys on our thoughts, desires, plans, relationships, health, faith, and so much more that is blind to the human eye. Through this journey with my son Carston, I endured attacks like these from every angle yet refused to give up any of my territory. It was the most challenging thing I've ever experienced, but let me ask you this: Would you sit by and allow an assassin to trick, threaten, or take out your child? Would you turn your head to an abductor attempting to steal your child away? No, of course not, because as parents, we'd bring out whatever weapon necessary to keep them safe. Similarly, in the spiritual realm, we have to fight against the predator, Satan, who is always lurking for an opportunity to strike because he is the assassin, the abductor.

"For though we live in the world,
we do not wage war as the world does.
The weapons we fight with
are not the weapons of the world.

On the contrary they have divine power
to demolish strongholds."

2 CORINTHIANS 10:3–4

To protect ourselves, and even our children, from the devil's lies, temptation, and control he so desperately thirsts for, we have to call on God every day. Through the Holy Spirit, our weapons of prayer, fasting, biblical truth, and worship are the only things that destroy evil forces. The crucifixion is what made these tools so powerful as the Lord Jesus arose from death, ascended to Heaven, and released His Holy Spirit to speak to us and help guide us in this life. As a believer in Jesus Christ, the Holy Spirit lives in me. This means I actively carry the same power that raised Jesus from the grave, and you can too (Ephesians 1:19–20). But deciding what you do with this power thereafter is crucial to advance in battle.

There is both struggle and triumph that comes with obedience to Christ when the enemy does strike. Trusting in God's full control over a life when all medical odds were against us was exhausting. Still, victory was only possible by releasing my flesh and acknowledging my own capabilities and ideas for what to do or what would work. As my son's condition was revealed, I asked

God, and God alone, to heal him, to re-create him from the inside out, and in return, I would testify about His miracles and give Him all glory for what He has done.

As I'm writing, I relive the supernatural fight over my son's life with every word, including original entries from my journal, descriptions of every medical finding, and tribulation before he was born and after. I've documented the incredible works of God with visions and signs He gave me throughout the assignment, not to mention the many lessons I've learned and still use today. It seems whenever we are faced with a trial, our souls naturally find worth in the result of our battle. Win or lose, we celebrate or grieve accordingly, but the ultimate value is not in the outcome—it's in the way we fight. We battle with perseverance, we believe without doubt, and we do all that is in our power to cast the enemy back to hell. Then and only then will we win, never looking back in regret, living a life full of purpose. This is my testimony.

CHAPTER I

Surrender It All

"Then I heard the voice of the Lord saying,
'Whom shall I send? And who will go for us?'
And I said, 'Here am I. Send me.'"

ISAIAH 6:8

T HE WINTER OF 2016 CHANGED THE COURSE OF MY LIFE FOREVER. From vacancy to overflow, God answered my prayer overnight. Having said that, I couldn't see the blessings or reap the fullness I'm living in now until all the trials in that season were finished. I'm about to unfold it all, but you have to know my heart was in a desperate place. Consumed by uncertainty all around me, I was done with the busyness of life and the dedication I was putting into my own endeavors. Nothing was filling me like I knew God could, so day and night, I pressed Him to reveal the greater things He had for my life. I could never have planned for His response to unfold so unpredictably, but I could sense His presence in it so strongly. Though it was the most difficult assignment I've ever endured, giving up was never an option for me. God heard my requests and answered time after time, empowering me in the face of opposition and replacing confidence in the office of fear that I visited so regularly. He showed me, through faith, who He created me to be—a warrior who can conquer anything with Him by my side. All doubts, every opinion, and impossibility—He has never lost a battle. Rising as the victor over it all, I'm ready to share my fight with the hope that you, too, will discover a strength you never knew you had.

This mission from God started with a new year and the greatest thirst for God that could not be quenched. I wanted to know God more and fall into Him with full obedience; however, looking ahead to an uncertain future was intimidating, and I wasn't sure how to prepare, how to advance. The previous five years had kept me so busy. Getting married and starting a life right out of high school was something I never expected, but these events were clear and crucial parts of God's plan to deepen my convictions and faith.

Our faith is the confidence we have in God on what we can't see but yet still believe He is doing in our lives (Hebrews 11:1). As an insecure child who grew up in two households, moving and changing schools multiple times, it was difficult for me to understand that God had a special design for my life and has a unique intention for every life. I found my identity in most of the wrong things. I knew God but grew to ignore Him and suffered because of it. Then I got married, and like any typical nineteen-year-old, I really didn't know what I was doing. By the grace of God, my husband became the stability I needed as we grew a life centered around God's presence. Marriage was a good challenge for those first five years. I finished my pastry degree, worked part-time, and renovated our first house top to bottom. Yes, it was overwhelming, but we were just kids. What did we know? In the middle of the chaos, we brought home our first baby girl, Trinity, a true joy that only God knew I would need for what was ahead.

As life settled down, the passion for my faith grew new and heavy, realizing my business kept me distracted from a deeper, more meaningful relationship with God. In fact, I had no idea what His purpose for my life even was. I was doing all the "righteous" things—attending and participating in church regularly, volunteering at church camp every summer, and maintaining my roles as a wife, chef, and mother. Surely all of these activities and roles should have defined or completed me in every way, but they didn't. We are supposed to be God's handiwork, created to accomplish the things He prepared in advance for us to do (Ephesians 2:10), but I couldn't let go of wondering what He had planned for me. Knowing I hadn't received a specific calling, the Holy Spirit within was shouting, "There is more!"

It was clear this void inside me needed a complete filling, so much so that I was up at random hours for several nights praying, "God, use me! Whatever you need, show me." I was so tired of entertaining anything else above God, and I knew I was hindering any advancement He had for my life by not giving Him enough of my time. This was a desperate cry out of true surrender. My intense desire to lay everything down became so powerful, and giving in and trusting God to sort it all out was my only option.

After many weeks of praying like this, it seemed like I got nothing from God, just nothing. My wait for His direction prolonged day after day, but still, I made God an even greater priority than He ever had been. In this time of pressing in, my words of prayer increased just the same, "What do you have for me, God, that is more than anything else I've ever done for You? Use my life to bring You glory; show me how!" My desires were His desires, to be used for His kingdom. I lived in full anticipation for His answer and was ready to work towards it. I found that surrendering to God is anything but a weakness; it provides the spiritual empowerment over all the unknowns, the key to the greater things.

Moving forward, still unassured of what to do at that time, I noticed a sick, nauseous feeling inside. My physical body was so weak, all I wanted to do was sleep. Pregnancy crossed my mind, although I didn't have the same signs I'd had with Trinity, so other concerns worried me, which led to an appointment with my family doctor. In the meantime, I decided to take the pregnancy test…and my fears turned into rejoicing! The voices in my head were speaking "depression" and "confusion," but God had plans for new life.

This was a huge moment for me spiritually. After asking God to use me, He delivered, and I mean literally. I had no idea then, but everything about my son's life was the answer to my prayers for a greater purpose. In my waiting, I couldn't see or understand what was happening in the spiritual realm, and at times I wondered if anything was happening at all. But God has the perfect timing and plan, even if it's not what we would choose ourselves. This journey through my pregnancy and son's life is something I would have not ever pictured for myself.

Only a couple of weeks later, I walked into the ultrasound room for the first time. With my heart pounding outside of my chest, all I could think about was my bloodwork that had come back a few days prior with high HCG levels. The room was silent, besides the searching sounds of the ultrasound machine. Seconds felt like minutes until we finally heard a heartbeat, and to my surprise, I was already fifteen weeks along. "It's a healthy baby boy!" the technician exclaimed.

I can still recall the pain in my cheeks from smiling so much that day. Justin and I tried to think of a name that evening, but it was evident we both had our own ideas. Justin has a soft spot for old-fashioned names like "Ford," but I had been cherishing the name "Carston" for years. When my research found that Carston meant "Christ-follower" in many languages, I couldn't budge; this name was the one. So we went back and forth until Justin finally gave in (thank you, Justin), and we agreed to name our sweet boy Carston Ford.

God was working to set this new course of my life in place. A baby always brings about change no matter who you are, but little did I know this blessing would become a very complicated solution to fill the emptiness and lack of purpose I was so desperate for. In fact, so much more was stripped from me before I ever felt the fullness God had in store. If I could have had even the slightest glimpse into the future, I would have stayed in that perfect moment, soaking up the simplicity of each day and every easy encounter God gave me with Him.

Things were about to change drastically. My life was still busy with the same routine, the same pace in relationship with God—reading my Bible, going to church, attending our small group, and praying and seeking God's purpose for this season of my life. It was all I knew to do, but still, I wasn't getting enough of Him. As I sought God to use me in greater ways, I felt the urge to give up even more of myself—my secrets, mistakes, thoughts, plans, and desires. He wanted access to every part of me, refining me further into His image each day. The thing is, to experience the fullness of God, He needs us to fully let go so that He can prepare everything within us for not only the blessings to come but for the battles to be waged by the enemy. Through our vulnerability with God, we make a way to be filled with the Holy Spirit, transformed into a spiritual warrior, and remaining in this stance is the key to surviving opposing threats. This is the place in my life, with many blessings and arms open wide to God, where I collided with my worst fears on uncharted territory as the enemy tried to take me out.

"Whether you turn to the right or to the left,
your ears will hear a voice behind you, saying,
'This is the way; walk in it.'"

ISAIAH 30:21

Unpredictable—My New Reality

At twenty-four weeks, I was feeling less sick and more hungry as each day went by. One night I stumbled downstairs to the kitchen for a snack, then to the bathroom and back to bed, my usual routine. But one night, something was different. As soon as I laid down, I felt this sudden wet sensation. My pajamas were wet and my bed, even. I thought, "Oh no! Did my water just break?" I woke Justin and rushed to the bathroom to see what was happening, but then the leaking stopped. I couldn't go back to sleep no matter how hard I tried, counting the hours until the OB office opened.

I called right at 8:00 a.m., needing answers. Instead, I got more questions. The nurse asked me how much fluid I had lost? When did it stop? Was I in any pain? Then after answering everything, she simply concluded that my bladder had leaked, which is quite common mid- to late-pregnancy.

I couldn't help but think she was totally wrong about me. I was hoping for an appointment, but before I could say anything, she tried reassuring me that if it were amniotic fluid, the leaking would not have stopped. She then directed me to call back for an office visit if this became a pattern. All of it didn't match up to my gut feeling, though. I remember sinking into the couch and simply shutting down what I truly felt inside. The enemy took my peace of mind and ability to stand up for myself, and I gave in. Instead of voicing my concerns, I felt powerless.

Through many life lessons now, I've learned that my gut feeling is the prompting of the Holy Spirit, and following it is critical if we are committed to letting God lead. His Spirit actually intertwines with ours so He can freely speak to us, able to deliver messages from Heaven at any moment. What we choose to do with His voice and hand in our lives is the expression of our faith. We can say we have faith but are we equipped to trust Him when it doesn't make sense? Believe Him during what seems like impossible circumstances? It depends on us to be ready for them, which takes diligence, preparation, and dedication. Romans 12:1–2 tells us to offer our bodies as a living sacrifice, holy and pleasing to God, to not conform to the pattern of this world but be transformed by the renewing of our minds. Then we will be able to test and approve what God's will is, which is so important to follow His direction instead of our own if we want His blessings to follow.

The more private time I spend with God, the more sure of His voice I become. As our relationship grows, the things I entertain myself with fade into the background, shifting more into things that bring me closer to Him. More Heaven and less World, whether it's friendships, TV shows, reading material, hobbies, or empty time. When I am obedient, God directs me back to His holiness. Being fueled with God's fire has given me the confidence to fight my battles by relying on the Holy Spirit as the Commander.

God continued warning me something was wrong, so I called back into the office a few days later like the nurse suggested and wound up sitting in the same ultrasound room more confused than ever. The tech didn't say anything as he was catching a glimpse of Carston. His whole demeanor was off compared to the chatty older man he was at my first visit. It's the OB's job to review ultrasound pictures and notify the patient with results, but I thought if he could say something good, he would have. Instead, he left me with nothing—not even a picture to take with me, and that's when I knew something was not right. What an understatement that was.

I got the call right in the rush of food prep at work. My OB's nurse urged me to get to Riverside Hospital because I had extremely low fluid around the baby. I wasn't sure what exactly that meant for Carston or me, so simple-mindedly, I asked her if I could at least finish my last hour at work, but she insisted I hurry, saying, "Your doctor has written on your chart ASAP! ASAP! ASAP!"

I called Justin at work that afternoon and left a message. My mom's family was on vacation, so his mom rode up with me and prayed the whole way there. Her knowledge about hospital stays stirred up courage within me, remembering how Justin's dad had fallen thirty feet and survived.

I signed in at labor and delivery, where they took all my information then placed me into a tiny room to be examined. Right away, I had an ultrasound taken by a resident; he was slow to speak, so Andrea insisted on knowing if the fluid was still low and what that meant for the baby and me. Before any direct answer, he called in another doctor, who also took an ultrasound, confirming only 1 cm of fluid surrounding Carston. She immediately diagnosed me with premature rupture of membranes, explaining how my amniotic sac had torn, causing the leak, something that would not stop and had to be taken seriously.

I understood all of this, which sounded fine initially until the registration lady came in with this standard paperwork for me to read and sign. As I began reading, I couldn't seem to accept in my mind that the papers demanded I be admitted there in the hospital on bed rest until I gave birth. I was in shock, and no words would come out, but my mind was spinning with several refusing thoughts. How could I have agreed with the sentence of hospital life for the next three months? I thought of Trinity, how she wouldn't understand, and who would take care of her? Who would take care of Justin, the house, our finances? I mean, who has three months to just lie in a bed and do nothing?

As my frustration simmered, I began to learn how serious it was, that, unlike a normal pregnancy where the water would break to indicate delivery, mine wouldn't be doing that. I had no fluid besides what my body was still trying to produce, which meant Carston could have come at any time with no warning. The doctor tried encouraging me, assuring me there were more mothers at the hospital in the same situation, and there was a support group that offered structured activities and counseling. I don't think I was quite ready to hear that. She mentioned how one mother's water broke at nineteen weeks, and she was thirty weeks then, living in the hospital waiting for her baby to come.

My mind was burning again, thinking, That's not going to be me! I just can't lie in a bed at the hospital for months, I just can't! I had no "proper" words to say; I had no clue what my options were or if I had any. Andrea filled in the blanks, asking, "Is there any way this could heal? Or is there a surgery to seal her membranes so she can go home? Could she have an in-home nurse stay at her house? Or could she just come to the hospital to be checked every day?"

The doctor's answer to anything and everything was simply "no," explaining, "We see women come in here frequently with ruptured membranes and no fluid but never get to go home until after they have their baby."

At that point, I could tell she was done arguing and ready to move on. Internally resistant but also helpless, I gave in and signed the papers. I was then moved into my permanent room, where a nurse started an IV of antibiotics to prevent any infection to baby Carston and myself. She gave me more information about my stay and that a 2-D ultrasound was scheduled for the next day to take a closer look at my fluid and fetal development.

Tuesday, June 16, 2016

I can't stop debating with God or wondering why I'm here. Unanswerable questions keep revolving as I try to figure out what's next on my own. How did this happen? How is anything going to be prepared for this baby? His room needs to be finished and decorated; I still have to buy crib sheets, blankets, boy clothes, a diaper bag, and everything that goes in it. I want more time to do things with just Trinity. So much is going to change and already has with no warning.

Here I am with no freedom, the medical world is so intimidating, as if all the facts and expectations they give are written in stone. It's been tested, it's been proven, there's no way around it, no way I can heal and go home. As badly as I want released, it seems like everything is working to keep me in this bed. It's time to rest, but I can't; time to accept this, but I won't.

My first mistake was giving the hospital physical authority to admit me and proceed with their wishes without recognizing God's power in the midst of my frustration. My selfishness opened gateway-after-gateway for the enemy to blur what I knew about God and how He works, elements of my mind the devil should never have had access to. We get that way sometimes, don't we? Consumed by the moment of only what we can see and make sense of, instead of using that energy to first consult with God, recognizing the fight against the enemy. Our self-pity hinders God's power, but emotions aside, we can access the Holy Spirit and His commands for battle at any time. Something seriously had to shift inside for me to realize I'm fully equipped for this fight. I am a living temple of the Holy Spirit, and God had been training me all that time leading up to this moment. If I was ever going to walk out of that hospital more healed and with more faith than I had come in with, it was time to snap out of my weakness and step into what I was created for. I am God's warrior.

ARTILLERY VAULT

Keep these verses at the ready for when you feel God calling you to surrender your will to His.

➤——➤ ISAIAH 6:8

➤——➤ EPHESIANS 2:10

➤——➤ ISAIAH 30:21

➤——➤ ROMANS 12:1–2

➤——➤ REVELATION 5:8

FAITH CHECKPOINT

*Search your heart and fortify the walls of your faith to
ensure security through the terrain of the unknown.*

Paying Attention to the Messenger

At times we get angry over our circumstances. We will be upset and not
always know the answer or solution, so we have to be ready. In faith, we have
to expect that God will raise us above the enemy's schemes. Surrendering
everything to God is Step One. Inviting the Holy Spirit into your life, if you
haven't already, and keeping God as your primary leader in life are the next
crucial actions. To stay focused and continually renew our minds, we have
to fill our spirit up with the things of God and allow His Spirit to guide us.
Church, Bible-time, small group, study apps, worship radio, and Christian
podcasts and books are great tools we can use to go deeper, but today I challenge you to spend even more time specifically in *prayer*. Quiet time with God
is really key, but you can actually communicate with Him easily throughout
your day as you work hard to complete your schedule. Not a single authentic
prayer goes unnoticed by God, whether the prayer is a quick conversation or
long, quiet moments spent with Him. To God, they all count!

In the Bible, John was given a revelation of the throne room where he saw
prayers being offered as incense before Jesus.

*"And when he took the scroll, the four living beings and the twenty-four
elders fell down before the Lamb. Each one had a harp, and they held
gold bowls filled with incense, which are the prayers of God's people."*

REVELATION 5:8 NLT

Literally, this is what happens in the spiritual realm. Our prayers are actions that move God's heart; they are tangible and very real. The amazing thing is God wants to respond. He uses the Holy Spirit to communicate back to us, so we can't afford to forfeit the time it takes to grow a relationship with Him.

Don't be surprised when Satan says, "Just give up. God doesn't care." He will try his hardest to get sin and shame between you and God or distract you with worldly pleasures when God-growth should be the priority. Satan tries to lessen your praying because he knows praying will lessen him. And he attempts to silence your worship because he knows worship will silence him. The devil wants nothing more than to keep you from building up these tools that will tear him down. So resist the temptation to quit. There is so much at stake. Our life's purpose, our response to the unknown, our hand in battle, all stem from our relationship with God. God's desire is to use each of us to advance His kingdom, and along the way, He wants to help us live victoriously through this life. With many blessings in store, if He calls you out, are you willing to obey? Are you ready to endure? As you take this challenge to amplify the Holy Spirit within you, rank up in faith and remember:

- Surrendering to God is anything but a weakness. Surrender is spiritual empowerment over all the unknowns, the key to the greater things.

- Through our vulnerability with God, we develop a willingness to be transformed into God's image and filled with the Holy Spirit. Remaining in this stance is key to surviving opposing threats.

- Our self-pity hinders God's power, but emotions aside, we can access the Holy Spirit and His commands for battle.

WEAPONS OF TRUTH

Who is the Holy Spirit, and how do we access Him?

Look up the following verses in your Bible and write down what they say. Spend a moment thinking about what each verse says about *prayer and the Holy Spirit*, specifically. How will you respond to these truths today?

PROVERBS 15:29

_____

_____

_____

_____

_____

JOHN 14:26

_____

_____

_____

_____

_____

Acts 2:38

_____

_____

_____

_____

_____

Romans 8:26

_____

_____

_____

_____

_____

ADDITIONAL NOTES:

_____

_____

_____

_____

_____

_____

_____

_____

CHAPTER 2

Ruler of the Battlefield

*"For the LORD your God is the one who goes with you to fight
for you against your enemies to give you victory."*

DEUTERONOMY 20:4

THEY SAY GOD GIVES THE HARDEST BATTLES TO HIS STRONGEST SOLDIERS. It's hard to accept that He welcomes specific challenges into our lives, but we can be assured it is not without a motive. Through this particular trial, my character and faith were altered forever. I'm now strong enough to face whatever else comes at me without the need for worry and confusion. Finally, I am living a life of true freedom. Choosing to let God go with you into battle will pull out things deep within you never knew you had, traits that strengthen your faith and build up His name and kingdom. Isn't this the point of this Christian life—to be a growing disciple of Christ?

I entered the fight of my life, totally unaware of what the enemy was scheming. I couldn't predict what would be next, no matter how hard I tried, but it was important for me to learn quickly that spiritual forces were behind it all.

"For our struggle is not against flesh and blood, but against the rulers, against the authorities, against the powers of this dark world and against the spiritual forces of evil in the heavenly realms."

EPHESIANS 6:12

The battle wasn't against a doctor or nurse; it wasn't a procedure or test to be angry with. It was the enemy using these people and things and my own fears to get to me. It was only through the Lord's stamina, courage, and security that I was able to stand firm and endure the next day and the next day as He fought on my behalf.

That first day of the battle was hard. I eventually broke through a firm wall I had built made up of only what I could comprehend, what I physically saw around me, which limited my actions for what could be next—my release from the enemy's grip and the hospital. I did do one thing right from the beginning, though: I refused to agree with this evil scheme over my body. Yes, the damage was proven by professionals, and I didn't doubt them at all, but spiritually, I wouldn't allow my physical brokenness to define me. I wouldn't accept this diagnosis to be all there was, but I didn't know what to do from there. I was simply refusing out of anger, not realizing the enemy was after me. I couldn't even think of how to retaliate, that is, until Pastor Tim Teague came to my room. He prayed for my healing and reminded me that even though it seemed like I had no rule, I always have spiritual authority as a believer in the Lord. I could lay there and choose to wallow in my fate, allowing the devil to reign over everything from my emotions to the physical ailments of my body, or I could sit enthroned next to the Father, who was actively pursuing my healing and release through Jesus Christ who made the ultimate way.

It wasn't an easy decision to surrender my mental ruling over my physical circumstance but to be released from the chaos, I knew I had to yield. I handed the entire situation over to God, realizing He had a purpose for everything, even my time there. God has a great way of calming, preparing, and strengthening us for what is to come. We need only to get out of our heads and into His presence to receive it. So that first night, I finally fell asleep feeling assured, knowing God had my back. I remember waking up revived, feeling positive, and believing with everything I had that we would see more fluid in my 2D ultrasound.

I sat back in the cold, plastic-covered chair, with Justin on my left and the monitor on my right, and I felt certain of my healing but was nervous for the proof to be discovered. The doctor came in, introducing herself, with her fancy diamond earrings, glasses, and curly hair pulled back in a ponytail. Following behind her were three younger gentlemen who managed to squeeze in beside us. The interns didn't bother me at first; they never said anything, even as she showed them exactly what to do. But I changed my mind on that later. As things started out, it didn't take long for her to report exactly what I'd been praying for, an obvious increase of fluid from 1 cm to 4 cm, which was just simply out of this world for me to witness. Clearly, even the smallest amount of faith gives God the opportunity to work.

Internally, I was rejoicing, and nothing could ruin that moment, that is, until the smiles on everyone's faces vanished. There was no easing into what was coming, and just like that, I was wrecked all over again. My doctor explained how they had detected many abnormalities in the "fetus." I clearly remember her saying "fetus" instead of referring to Carston as a baby. The terminology bothered me so much. He was living and growing, much more than just an object—he was my baby. She didn't speak any life with her words, only science, and as she continued, the room grew to be so cold. They couldn't find his stomach; only one-and-a-half kidneys were present; there was unknown tissue in the lungs, plus they detected a heart defect, clenched fists, and a clubfoot. She went on talking about how life could be incompatible, especially if this was caused by a suspected genetic disorder called Trisomy 18.

It was all so nonchalantly spoken over me, just another day at work for her. I get it. But was it really necessary to have an audience staring right at me as the worst news of my entire life was rolled out to obliterate me? I was frozen stiff, unwilling to absorb any of her thoughts and predictions as she carried on. I was hearing it but couldn't wrap my mind around it. Trisomy 18? I couldn't even pronounce it.

Wasting no time, she immediately requested my permission to test for the probability of the diagnosis being true. This is done by either drawing amniotic fluid from around the baby to test their DNA, which is 98% accurate, or blood can be drawn from the mother and tested by separating her chromosomes from the babies, which is only 25% accurate. At the time, these words and numbers were all mixed up in my head. Nothing was clear, but it didn't really matter because I only had one option under my condition—4 cm of fluid around Carston was still not enough for it to be drawn and tested. She elaborated on the importance of the blood test, but on top of it all, she made abortion a clear and reasonable choice. "Termination of the pregnancy" were her exact words, making it sound so simple, like it could all just be over, finished. I knew it was the doctor's duty to give me all the options, stressing how these findings could make life so hard for Carston and me, but it seemed as if she were trying to convince me to end things when there was still so much time for him to grow and change.

The hard truth is, as much as I wanted all of this to go away, nothing just disappears by the casting down of another's life, whether by eliminating someone's physical existence or destroying them internally by our actions and words. These are plots of the enemy. Second Corinthians 11:14 explains how Satan disguises himself as an angel of light. We have to be careful of the devil pretending to be good, as he knows what pleases our flesh and will not hesitate to prey on it, to satisfy us at the moment, only for potential consequences to later arise.

And so there I was, a tiny speck backed into the corner of a room that became a giant engulfing me. The enemy was blowing up each word the doctor spoke, not even trying to disguise himself now, just straight up trying to take me out. Although I remained in faith, I felt each piercing. I was living through a reality that we are not immune to pain every time we choose faith. I knew God's character was to work it all out in the end, but I wasn't feeling the goodness right then. The doctor was simply ready for an answer to move forward, but I just didn't have one. With so much to bear all at once, it was impossible to fully understand everything. Justin, who had been quietly sitting with me the whole time, broke his silence, grabbed my hand, and pulled me out of the room. We endured the same heartache, but no words would come out as he wheeled me back to my room in silence and devastation.

We were given space to process the news, and my doctor came by later that evening to discuss things further. She started again with Trisomy 18, which meant that every cell within Carston's body had three copies of the eighteenth chromosome instead of two. She stressed its ability to cause complications with his development in the womb and life after birth. It is a rare condition—it only occurs in 1 of every 6,000 live births, and for some reason, it had to be my son. Even worse, 50% of those babies are stillborn, and approximately 10% survive one year of life. On top of it all, baby girls have higher rates of live births than baby boys; it seemed like nothing was in our favor. Justin and I never spoke the words, but we both knew aborting Carston was not going to happen no matter what they found. It made me sick hearing the odds so greatly stacked against him, as though he had no chance. I couldn't live with being the one to take his life, to deny him the opportunity to try, and at the same time, I would have sacrificed my life just to give him one of normalcy. I was so numb, and my body tingled off and on, taking it in and crying it out.

"The LORD will fight for you;
you need only to be still."

EXODUS 14:14

God's Strategy Prevails in Battle

I couldn't tell you then why this was happening to my little boy who was so helpless, who did nothing wrong. I hated thinking about it, so I tried blocking out every emotion that tore at me. I even tried to get rid of comforting thoughts. It was easier just to remain broken, but the lump in my throat that night was just as real as God's voice telling me I had to believe what He says more than how I felt. He didn't abandon me there; He was still fighting for me.

I laid in that hospital bed, realizing no one in there could change my situation; only God had the power to heal Carston.

"Trust in the LORD with all your heart
and lean not on your own understanding;
in all your ways submit to him,
and he will make your paths straight."

PROVERBS 3:5–6

For Carston, I had no time to mess around and waste energy on thoughts that were getting me nowhere. I had to fall into God and let Him war for me. To be honest, if it were only me suffering, would I have so quickly come out of my depression? Probably not, but when our children's lives are at stake, it triggers a mother's response. So my selfish cries turned into shouting and calling for more help from his Creator. I begged and begged for God's healing, and what I didn't know then was that Justin was begging too. He was driving home late from the hospital when a car swerved right in front of him, drawing his attention to the license plate, which read "GODNCTRL." It was the direct sign from Heaven we desperately needed, God's voice so tangible, securing the unknowns with His promises.

Our decision to fight for Carston didn't sit well with the devil; he was losing the fight over my mind, and he tried about anything to get me back into his dark place. The next morning started with a nurse who came in to check on my IV. She didn't hold back her opinion at all, saying, "You have your whole life ahead of you. Why ruin it?" I couldn't believe her boldness, but I just nodded as though I understood what she was saying, and I did. My mind and spirit had me going back and forth between the anger of this reality and God's purpose for it. Although I was counting on God to help my son, I still had emotions. It's totally human of us to "feel" as long as we don't fight from them. These medical professionals were not viewing my situation through the same lens, through the direction of the Holy Spirit. When we rely on the fix-it ability of people who give their best knowledge, it can limit our transforming trust in God, who makes a way when there is no way. Recognizing this made it easier to dismiss the negativity, leaving room in my head and heart to hear what God wanted me to do.

Thankfully, Justin and Trinity brought me a fragment of normalcy during my stay. Trinity, only being two years old, could tell something was wrong even when I wasn't teared up. She would ask, "You have boo-boos?" and say, "Don't worry, Mommy." Her words served as a warm hug that would never let go, and don't get me started on the real hugs. I was able to almost forget about all the bad things swirling around me; that is, until the nurse pushed the dreaded wheelchair into my room for every new test and observation, a constant reminder I was still not considered well.

Thursday, June 16, 2016

In the ultrasound this afternoon, we looked more closely at Carston's brain and found more unexpected news that crushed me. Now missing tissue on both sides and back of Carston's brain, and no cerebellum at all. They told me the cerebellum receives information from the sensory systems and regulates motor movements, including posture, balance, coordination, and speech. These words could have killed me.

I can't physically fix this. It's so frustrating, but I'm letting God take it and just trying not to feel. I couldn't help but smile, though, when I found out my fluid went from four centimeters to eleven. Ironically enough, this morning was the first time I woke up dry, not leaking any fluid at all. I thought it was just coincidence, but when the doctor confirmed these results, I knew I was healed!

Miracle #1

Membranes sealed at 27 weeks.
Amniotic fluid increase from 4 cm to 11 cm!

News of the increase in amniotic fluid left Justin, and I more speechless than we've ever been. After all we'd had to endure, the punches to the gut, we didn't want that moment of victory to ever leave. We were shocked to see that the doctor was excited too. She wanted to perform the amino test now that there was enough fluid, so I let her. A more accurate test seemed like the right thing to do, even though I was nervous about it.

Within the same room, she prepped everything and began the procedure right then and there. I remember being lightheaded watching the whole thing under ultrasound. The six-inch needle punctured my uterus, drawing vile after vile of amniotic fluid right beside Carston's head. I was beginning to regret the decision I made, clenching the armrests and wanting to say something, but I thought I might make her mess up. Thankfully, she finished quickly, and the procedure was a success.

Overthinking everything again. I remember asking Justin why God healed me and didn't re-create the organs and DNA my son so desperately needed. It was rhetorical, but Justin broke through my descending thoughts, reminding me of the Bible story of Joshua. Although the Jordan River stopped flowing instantly for the Israelites to pass through, they still had to march around the walls of Jericho for seven days as God supernaturally fought for them, and then they came down. In the same way, this battle we were facing was not ours to physically fight. It was hard to come to terms with this being out of my control and not knowing how long it may take to see God's miracles revealed. But no matter what, I had no choice other than to endure and believe.

The fetal heart echo was the last thing scheduled that day, and to my relief, the cardiologist from Nationwide Children's Hospital explained everything in detail. He drew me a picture of a normal heart and one of Carston's. A normal heart is made of four chambers; the top two are the atrium, and the bottom two are ventricles. The problem with Carston's heart was that the bottom left ventricle was so small, he predicted it would shrink and be totally gone by birth. The left ventricle is the thickest of all the chambers and is responsible for pumping oxygenated blood to tissues all over the body. Reiterating Carston's incompatibility with life, he explained that this would make life near impossible.

On top of this, Carston's aorta was connected to the right ventricle instead of the left, preventing proper blood and oxygen flow to the rest of his body, which is called a double outlet right ventricle. Luckily, this is fixable through surgery but wasn't necessary right away for Carston because he had a hole between the bottom two chambers allowing the blood to flow through the left and out the right side. The heart defects were expected to change as he continued to grow and develop, which would determine the course of action taken after birth, "If he can even survive the birthing process," the cardiologist said. I just loved how he threw that in there.

I was literally learning a whole different language. Pronouncing these diagnoses, along with understanding what everything meant and factoring in the unknowns, was overwhelming. A lot of it made no sense, and the hopeless tones didn't make me want to find out more. It was near impossible to stay positive being surrounded by "experts" with no inspiration for growth and change. In that meeting, I held onto the fact that God formed Carston's heart with a hole that already allowed blood flow. In my mind, He was still in control.

They scheduled another ultrasound, heart echo, and a fetal MRI to look closer at Carston's brain for three weeks later, on July 7. When we made it back to my room, the nurse came in with some papers, and that was the last of everything. Miraculously, I was discharged. There was much more going on than the human eye could see. The doctors called it a "medical mystery," but we were positive my healing was a miracle from God, the first of many. Several nurses and hospital staff asked how I could seem at peace through this, which made it evident that my faith was on display, believing in life when abortion and lack of life were on the tip of every doctor's tongue. Falling into God in weakness and pain is what removed me as an obstacle initially, allowing God to proceed with this victory on my behalf with more victories to come.

I would have been in the hospital for the following three months or until I delivered, but my total hospital stay was only three days, June 14 to 16. Although the future was unknown, we left that place with our heads held high, giving thanks to our God. It was hard, but I praised Him in my waiting and uncertainties. Many days were to come where more results and appointments built anticipation to witness God's movement.

ARTiLLERY VAULT

Keep these verses at the ready for when you need
confidence in God calling the shots.

- ➤ DEUTERONOMY 20:4
- ➤ EPHESIANS 6:12
- ➤ 2 CORINTHIANS 11:14
- ➤ EXODUS 14:14
- ➤ PROVERBS 3:5–6
- ➤ ISAIAH 41:10
- ➤ ISAIAH 55:8
- ➤ DEUTERONOMY 3:22

"So do not fear, for I am with you; do not be dismayed, for I am your God. I will
strengthen you and help you; I will uphold you with my righteous right hand."

ISAIAH 41:10

FAITH CHECKPOINT

*Search your heart and fortify the walls of your faith to
ensure security through the terrain of the unknown.*

It's God's Battle to Fight

Without our trials, would we ever get desperate for God? We need Him in the good times, and especially the bad. He never fails. God never loses a battle! And the thing is, this trial we keep claiming to be our own is actually His to begin with. He is the Commander here. The Bible tells us time and time again that God is fighting for us (Deuteronomy 3:22). He goes before us in battle. Through the Holy Spirit, He will give us the actions to take, if any at all. Sometimes He calls us to just be still, to keep the faith, which can be harder than actually doing something. We have to realize this because our own strategies are influenced by the flesh and will keep us spinning in circles, but only God's strategies will bring the everlasting victory.

During times when you are unable to process thoughts, and you are in pain and without hope, it only takes one encounter with God to get you out of your dark place. If you truly believe God is fighting for you and working through you, then there is nothing to fear. It helps me by picturing Him waiting for me right in my room, and He's waiting for you to acknowledge Him and believe in His way through the storm. I love how Isaiah 55:8 says, "For my thoughts are not your thoughts, neither are your ways my ways." It's not our job to understand how God operates or how He has the power to do the impossible. When we choose to believe without any logic or need for explanation, God will give us what we need internally and even what we need in the physical world to carry on to victory.

What is it that you are facing and overthinking as you attempt to find peace? I encourage you to put aside your own efforts today, as good as they may be. Drop them and choose faith, God's power, and His plan. Let Him know that you believe the battle is His. The Lord Himself will fight for you. You have the advantage, so rank up in faith and remember:

- Relying on the fix-it ability of people who give their best knowledge can limit your transforming trust in God, who makes a way when there is no way.

- Falling into God in weakness and pain removes us as an obstacle, allowing God to proceed with the victory on our behalf.

- Even the smallest amount of faith gives God the opportunity to work, giving attention to what He says over how we feel.

WEAPONS OF TRUTH

How do we know God is in control?

Look up the following verses in your Bible and write down what they say. Spend a moment thinking about what each verse says about *God's reign and sovereignty,* specifically. How will you respond to these truths today? Write it down.

ISAIAH 14:24

_____

_____

_____

_____

_____

JEREMIAH 32:17

_____

_____

_____

_____

_____

MATTHEW 10:29–31

_____

_____

_____

_____

_____

COLOSSIANS 1:16–17

_____

_____

_____

_____

_____

ADDITIONAL NOTES:

_____

_____

_____

_____

_____

_____

_____

_____

CHAPTER 3

Orders of Obedience

"Have I not commanded you?
Be strong and courageous.
Do not be afraid, do not be discouraged,
for the Lord your God will be with you wherever you go."

JOSHUA 1:9

H OME FELT SO GOOD. I was released from the hospital, and all it took was for me to give up my own thoughts and efforts, allowing God to step into my situation and radically change it. I decided to believe He could do it, and He did.

There is nothing special about me; in fact, I've often felt commonly misunderstood and unimportant, but my "not enough" set me apart and set up God's power to be revealed. He gave me the greatest form of acknowledgment I had ever received. He heard my every prayer and responded, releasing me to step outside and breathe the fresh air, to simply step and not be confined to a chair with wheels and a bed with rails. The sun took the place of fluorescent lights; birds were chirping instead of beeping machines; peace, calm, and warmth surrounded me. I didn't know what I had until it was gone.

I would have missed months of church being cooped up in the hospital, but that wasn't God's plan. Clearly, nothing is impossible for Him. I was determined to receive healing for my son, and that Sunday back was the first of many encounters when I met God at the altar for exactly that. The Lord's Spirit was ever-present and powerful among the entire sanctuary, and worship could not be stopped. There was a guest speaker who had come all the way from Alaska, and instead of preaching his planned message, he shared something God had placed on his heart right then. As he started speaking, I couldn't believe it—another reminder of Joshua's journey. He explained how the Israelites were not just marching for seven days but worshiping and praying around Jericho's walls. They were obedient, acting on what God instructed them to do so He could utilize His power and mighty hand over their battle. This lesson became my foundation to keep marching forward, believing in the miracle for my son no matter how long it took.

The guest pastor went on to preach that he had a word for someone specific in the church and decided to share a personal testimony. His son had medical issues that the doctor couldn't diagnose, and he was about to die as a young boy. He prayed and prayed for his son from the start of the complications. Then at midnight, he woke up beside his son's hospital bed feeling that God was telling him to dance right then and there in the hospital, so he did. The next day, the doctors noticed improvements, so they ran more tests, and miraculously, they found the boy healed! He emphasized how important it is to submit yourself to Christ, doing whatever He calls you to do, even if it's as crazy as dancing at midnight. We then diligently watch and pray because we do not know the time when God will act (Mark 13:33). At any second in our surrender and obedience, we can be the recipient of a miracle. God's orders overcome all physical circumstances, re-creating impossible to obtainable.

Towards the end of the sermon, the guest pastor requested for anyone seeking a miracle to come forward for prayer, so Justin and I walked up together. Pastor Teague anointed me, claiming Carston's healing. The guest pastor encouraged everyone to listen to God, and if He is saying to be different in prayer or worship, we need to put our pride aside and do it! As he spoke, I could feel right then that God was calling me to pray, not like I usually did, but on my knees, bowing down, giving up everything for our son to be healed. So from that point on, that's what took place in my quiet time, every morning and every night on my knees, pleading and praying for God to re-create the parts of Carston that needed His powerful touch.

It was no coincidence that God brought the story of Joshua to my attention two times within a week, and He wasn't finished yet. Two weeks after my discharge from Riverside, a call from the hospital came in. It was the geneticist reporting the results of the amino test being positive for Trisomy 18. How many times could a mother's heart break? Even though I was informed of this diagnosis being a great possibility, it still struck me hard because the whole time in waiting I was gearing up for a miracle. I immediately felt sick. Within that diagnosis, it sealed upon him the medical facts and statistics that came with it, and somehow, it all became our official reality.

I felt utterly destroyed all morning, but I knew I couldn't stay in that place—I wasn't giving up. I couldn't form many words of my own, so I prayed a verse that I knew well using 2 Timothy 1:7 as my guide, "God, allow your Spirit of power, love, and a sound mind to overcome any spirit of fear within me. Dissolve any false emotion that tries to control me." Then I opened my Bible to Joshua chapter 1, but before I could read a single word, my ceiling fan flipped the pages to Joshua chapter 3, so I began right where I felt God had led me.

And the LORD said to Joshua, "Today I will begin to exalt you in the eyes of all Israel, so they may know that I am with you as I was with Moses"… Now the Jordan is at flood stage all during harvest. Yet as soon as the priests who carried the ark reached the Jordan and their feet touched the water's edge, the water from upstream stopped flowing. It piled up in a heap a great distance away, at a town called Adam in the vicinity of Zarethan, while the water flowing down to the Sea of the Arabah (that is, the Dead Sea) was completely cut off. So the people crossed over opposite Jericho. The priests who carried the ark of the covenant of the LORD stopped in the middle of the Jordan and stood on dry ground, while all Israel passed by until the whole nation had completed the crossing on dry ground.

JOSHUA 3:7, 15–17

Just like that, my burden was lifted. After reading this inspiration from Heaven, I was overwhelmed and could only wonder, who am I that God would care to keep reassuring me over this battle I faced? As worship music played in my room, the lyrics of a favorite song caught my ear, reminding me, God had split the sea for even me, so I could walk right through my battle, drowning all my fear in His perfect love along the way. And in amazement, I just bawled, knowing right then that God was moving and making a way through my impossible circumstance.

"There is no fear in love, but perfect love drives out fear."

1 JOHN 4:18

Loyalty's Advantage

God wants to see that we are as dedicated to victory His way, in the challenges He tests us with, as much as in our time of miracles. Sometimes He takes us to places we've never been and asks us to do things we've never done, which makes us uncomfortable, fearful even, but this is the training we need to rank up in our faith to conquer what lies ahead. God called me out, way out, of my natural private time with Him and asked me to open my mouth on His behalf. What would you do if God asked you to share what's been going on in your life, to tell of the things He's told you in private? God was surely pushing me out of my comfort zone spiritually and physically in this season. He came through in a huge way for me, so now it was time to show Him how serious I was about letting Him lead.

It all began with the major tests I'd had at Children's and Riverside Hospital for my twenty-eight-week checkup. Everything about an MRI seemed intimidating and unsettling, which turned out to be true, but was necessary so we could look closer at Carston's brain. The room was freezing cold, and the thin gown they had me wear wasn't helping. I laid down on the board and slowly merged into the tube where only six inches of space remained from my face to the top closure. The nurse noticed me panicking and tried coaching me through it, reminding me, "Take deep breaths and keep your eyes closed, dear."

I carried on by whispering admissions to God about my fears and asking Him to help me get through them. I reassured myself that it would be good for Carston, and really it was too late to change my mind then anyway.

Throughout the test, the machine would not stop screeching. About half-way through the MRI, I felt a strong pain and push in my lower abdomen. I had no idea what it was or if Carston was okay. Even though an MRI is supposed to be totally safe, something just didn't feel right; all I could do in that dark tunnel was pray even harder for God's protection over him.

I couldn't get out of there and over to Riverside fast enough. I wanted to see Carston and get my MRI results, but it turned out that his heart echo was first on the agenda. The cardiologist was a different doctor than the last one I'd seen, and we talked through the whole thing. Surprisingly, he seemed concerned for my overall wellbeing, asking how I was coping with all this news that seemed to come out of nowhere?

I hesitated to answer, wondering how I could ever educate or share this testimony with people smarter than me or have questions I can't answer. Will I be judged because what I'm expecting is impossible, crazy even? I wanted to be so bold about the miracles we believed we'd receive instead of allowing my insecurities and fear of controversy to quiet my voice. To my very core, I knew if I didn't call on a higher power, my son would be left broken and declared everything the medical world had found him to be—hopeless. My God was in the midst of this, and I physically felt the responsibility of His power, knowing if He continued to heal, He expected me to testify. It seemed like a task I was incredibly unqualified for, but my spirit conquered my flesh, and its call came pouring out in one breath. I told the cardiologist everything, from God healing my membranes to the things I was counting on Him to do for my son.

I can still envision the very skeptical look on his face, probably more concerned about my "mental" wellbeing than before he initially asked that question. He replied with an elongated "Okayyy" under his breath, which totally rubbed me the wrong way. This was the reaction I feared. I wondered why my healing wasn't enough in that instant to prove God as my defender in this battle. Sure, it would have been much easier to just give up hope and accept this tragedy, then we would have all been on the same page, sharing the same sad looks and conversations, further digging a deeper hole to bury me in, but that's not what God called me to do.

Certainly, these medical findings were accurate, but they were also fiery arrows the enemy waged against me. There is absolutely nothing on Earth that we can place our hope in to deliver miracles. So many people are deceived and blinded by the enemy, who keeps them without faith. But the blood of the Lamb and the word of our testimony overcomes the enemy (Revelation 12:11). We can plant a seed of faith in unbelievers through sharing what God has done for us. So even with the doctor's negative response, I was serving my purpose then; however, I had no idea what was to come next.

The cardiologist took a few minutes to study Carston's images, and then he remarkably explained to us that the left bottom chamber of Carston's heart had not gotten smaller as first predicted. If his heart stayed in that condition, he could live for weeks or months before needing surgery, he admitted. We were so relieved and happy for Carston, but it was evident that the whole point was for me to overcome my fear by witnessing to this man. I believe it was through my obedience that I conquered the enemy and thus received a good report about Carston's heart.

There was a mixture of joy and anxiety beginning to rise as I knew my maternal-fetal medical doctor was going to be the one to enter next—the doubting one who so graciously discovered Carston's complications and inferred that ending his life was an easy thing that can be done. Although I couldn't wait to see Carston, I really didn't want to endure another heavy conversation with her. I knew her job was to present the facts and not get emotionally invested, but my goodness, the words she said before broke me. I took a lot of deep breaths in and deep breaths out. She began with the MRI results. To my surprise and hers, she lit up a half-smile saying, "The missing cerebellum HAS NOW APPEARED!"

Miracle #2

God crafted the missing cerebellum and tissue in Carston's brain.

*"And my God will meet all your needs
according to the riches of his glory in Christ Jesus."*

PHILIPPIANS 4:19

I was amazed. We couldn't have asked for anything more, and I couldn't help but tell her it was exactly what I'd been praying for and believing in. With no response (I wasn't expecting one), we moved onto the final procedure of the day, my ultrasound, which brought yet another concern to light.

Thursday, July 7, 2016

Carston seemed so perfect on the monitor today; his growth rate is average, 14 inches long and a little over 2 pounds, right where he should be, which made me feel like I had a normal baby for a second, just a normal mother with a normal baby at a routine exam. But I was brought back to reality with the mention of his remaining complications. I should be accustomed to it now, but it still feels so foreign to me; his brokenness is not what I want to hear, and I feel so strongly it's not what God wants me to approve of. Plus the fact that Carston's head is now up instead of head down makes me a little on edge. I now know that was the painful move he made during the MRI.

Literally with every good thing discovered, the enemy adds a new weight to my shoulders. I don't doubt that God intentionally created him like this, God doesn't make mistakes, for God is life and wants life for Carston. It's complicated to sort out all my thoughts about it, impossible to fully understand the big picture, but letting the Holy Spirit lead in my beliefs and actions is somehow the only thing that makes sense right now. I have to fight for life and the possibilities of healing that God can bring.

Today I was affirmed in a healing confirmation that my fluid is still normal, my first miracle. No matter what, I will remain patient and uncompromised in the Lord, I will mount up with wings like eagles, I will run and not be weary, I will walk and not grow faint (Isaiah 40:31). I will believe this until God's work in Carston is finished.

Through every challenge, God equipped me with what I needed to conquer my insecurities and fear, to break through what would have held me back from the greater things God wanted for Carston and me. Whether it was a Bible verse, message, or song, He provided the weapons and challenged me to act according to the prompting of the Holy Spirit. My faith-stretch was God's game plan to defeat the enemy's tactics and bondage over my son, something I had to recognize moving forward as things became more unclear and critical decisions weighed so heavy on my heart and mind.

ARTILLERY VAULT

Keep these verses at the ready for when God is calling you to obedience.

➤——→ JOSHUA 1:9

➤——→ MARK 13:33

➤——▷ 2 TIMOTHY 1:7

➤——▷ JOSHUA 3:7, 15–17

➤——→ 1 JOHN 4:18

➤——→ REVELATION 12:11

➤——▷ PHILIPPIANS 4:19

➤——▷ ISAIAH 40:31

➤——▷ JEREMIAH 1:4–8

FAITH CHECKPOINT

Search your heart and fortify the walls of your faith to
ensure security through the terrain of the unknown.

Beyond Your Hiding Place

Our faith expands when we allow the Holy Spirit to stretch us outside of our comfort zones. We know it as being uncomfortable, but in that feeling, something transformative happens when we let go of our physical cares and thoughts, doing what God calls us to do anyway. We step into the spiritual realm already a champion. In obedience, we win because we are pairing with God, who has all knowledge about what is happening and what's to come. He guides us victoriously to the space where we see Him do more than what we ever thought He could within our circumstance.

The word of the LORD came to me saying, "Before I formed you in the womb
I knew you, before you were born I set you apart; I appointed you as a prophet
to the nations." "Alas, Sovereign LORD," I said, "I do not know how to speak;
I am too young." But the LORD said to me, "Do not say, 'I am too young.' You
must go to everyone I send you to and say whatever I command you. Do not be
afraid of them, for I am with you and will rescue you," declares the LORD.

JEREMIAH 1:4–8

Wherever God has you today, don't forget how capable you are of accepting the good works and tasks in front of you. In your obedience, stay on guard and full of prayer, as the enemy will not stop trying to turn your situation into fear. He twists what we know as the truth into lies, festering them into relevant blockades of the future; that's what he's great at, deception. He wants us to get in the way of ourselves. Personally, I can handle outside jabs and battles of the world, but when my mind starts overthinking, that's the death of me. I praise God that He gave us His Holy Spirit. Through our obedience, we activate this greater force to overcome the devil's tactics against our minds and circumstance.

God overcame the physical truth of Mary being a virgin and used her to carry Jesus. He overcame the physical truth of David being a boy and enabled him to kill the giant Goliath. God overcame the truth of Lazarus, who was physically dead for three days but still healed him. Jesus worked miracles in the Bible-times and overcame many obvious physical traits within the lives of the people. He is so clearly still working within us the same way today. What about you? What is God calling you to do? In obedience, you will be stepping into the spiritual purpose God has for your life. As you rank up in faith, remember:

- Our "not enough" sets us apart and sets up God's power.

- God's orders overcome all physical circumstances, re-creating impossible to obtainable.

- Our faith-stretch is God's game plan to defeat the enemy.

WEAPONS OF TRUTH

What does God promise when we obey Him?

Look up the following verses in your Bible and write down what they say. Spend a moment thinking about what each verse says about *God's promises around obedience,* specifically. How will you respond to these truths today? Write it down.

DEUTERONOMY 5:33

_____

_____

_____

_____

_____

PROVERBS 16:20

_____

_____

_____

_____

_____

PSALM 34:9–10

_____

_____

_____

_____

_____

JOHN 14:21

_____

_____

_____

_____

_____

ADDITIONAL NOTES:

_____

_____

_____

_____

_____

_____

_____

_____

_____

CHAPTER 4

Aligning Faith with God's Will

"Father if you are willing,
take this cup from me;
yet not my will, but yours be done.'
An angel appeared to him
and strengthened him."

LUKE 22:42–43

W ITHIN OUR WAITING, MY ARMY WAS BUILDING IN THE SPIRITUAL
REALM. Many churches were praying for us, even some who didn't
know me, which humbled me so much. I'm still in awe at the countless prayer
warriors who interceded on my behalf and believed in a miracle for my son. I
wasn't sure why they cared so much, but I realize now God placed each one of
them in my path; each prayer was needed to go up and fight this battle.

Along with the many individuals who connected with me through social media, there wasn't a single Sunday where the Holy Spirit didn't move on my behalf with several anointings, and prayer people gathered around me. One morning, in particular, I received prayer from a man battling deadly cancer. He felt led by the Holy Spirit to give me further reassurance that Carston will be healed, just like he was. Many others joined in praying that day as well, and a friend of ours witnessed four angels among us as we were all crying out to God for my son's life. God would not stop proving how He was in this battle with us. It was incredible. I felt certain the angels were there that day to represent God's protection over Carston and to uplift me.

"For he will command his angels concerning you
to guard you in all your ways;
they will lift you up in their hands,
so that you will not strike your foot against a stone.
You will tread on the lion and the cobra;
you will trample the great lion and the serpent.
'Because he loves me,' says the Lord,
'I will rescue him; I will protect him,
for he acknowledges my name.'"

PSALM 91:11–14

A Collision of Science and Faith

At Carston's thirty-two-week ultrasound, his growth rate was still average, weighing in at 3.75 pounds and around 16 inches long, but somehow he was still breech. Additionally, my doctor detected one extra centimeter of fluid than normal, saying it didn't make her very happy. I still wonder what she meant by that because I never did ask. I was sick of the negative talk and convinced myself that God had placed the extra fluid there to give Carston room to flip around. Time was running out, and I began praying even harder for Carston, for him to flip and for God to restore and re-create what was broken. The enemy was not letting up, but neither was my army.

I remember walking up the stairs to the care conference, not knowing what to expect. I anticipated meeting the professionals who would be taking care of Carston at birth and through infancy, but again it was another reminder of Carston's reality and how everything would soon be coming to a head. Stepping into the conference room was intimidating; everything was white—the walls, the table, the doctors' clothes, and their thick binders, but I held my own and showed no external sign of wavering.

They each introduced themselves, giving their name, occupation, and passion for what they do. There were OB doctors and NICU doctors from Riverside, two NICU doctors from Children's Hospital, an RN, and also a chaplain. The chaplain started our conversation by asking what my thoughts and wishes were for Carston. Although I didn't share it aloud, my initial thought was, Will I be wasting my breath? Would they judge my testimony and beliefs as nonsense? In retaliation to my negative thoughts, I stepped out in faith, sharing how Justin and I had both been praying for a miracle; there was nothing else I could have said, as anything else would have been a lie. Thankfully, it turned out to be a much-needed breakthrough moment with the possibility for science and faith to coexist.

The room was silent, but I noticed a few smiles, which turned into uplifting comments. Compassion from each one reassured me that they are simply human, too, something I had to remember for later encounters in my journey with Carston's doctors. Our small talk was nice, but it came to a swift end. We were there to discuss how to physically treat Carston, not how God would save him, which would have been a much more productive meeting for me.

They started by presenting many possibilities that could happen at Carston's birth, most of which were impossible for me to entertain; I don't know how any mother could. One major concern was that he could have trouble breathing due to the unknown spot on his lung, so in this instance, how far would we want medical intervention, if any at all?

"What can we say to these things?
If God is for us, who can be against us?"

ROMANS 8:31 ESV

It was easy for us to say we wanted Carston to have life, but apparently, there were consequences if we chose to help him survive; things doctors could try at birth that would work for the moment, but long-term could leave him on machines for the rest of his life. Then they gave us the option of comfort care, just letting him pass away in our arms once he was born. Could you imagine looking down at your precious baby so helpless and simply holding back the care that he needs because you're too afraid of the unknown? They went on about several other plans and possibilities, needing answers to all of their questions, which were impossible to even process at the moment.

If your baby would be born alive, would you give us permission to intubate or use CPAP to assist breathing?

Do you agree with the long-term effects and outcomes of life with these machines?

Do you mind if your baby has a feeding tube, possibly forever?

Are you fully aware that not every complication and disability can be predicted with Trisomy 18, that by not choosing comfort care, we are deciding to pursue the unknown full of risks?

Would you further consider a DNR order, as resuscitating a patient with many complications can bring them back in worse condition?

Would you like to seek counsel with a chaplain on staff before and after birth?

And lastly,

Would you like a bereavement photographer at the birth?

Yes, they said bereavement, as though they were already planning for our baby to die. It was so tough hearing this. The meeting came to an end with the reminder that if Carston was still breach one month before delivery, a C-section would be scheduled at my next appointment, September 1.

"There are many possible risks with a C-section, a lot could go wrong but most likely wouldn't," an OB said, which gave me so much reassurance—ugh, not. Satan was surely trying to defeat me with the fact that something unpredictable was bound to happen, which I knew, but that meeting put a magnifying glass on it all. Those couple hours were tough to endure, but surprisingly, we ended the meeting with every head bowed in prayer as Carston's life hung in the balance.

"But you, when you pray, go into your inner room, close your door and pray to your Father who is unseen, and your Father who sees what is done in secret will reward you."

MATTHEW 6:6

Lord, Give Me a Sign

Two weeks went by where I didn't feel any strong movement from Carston; the C-section crept up in the back of my mind. My expectations and beliefs were challenged as time went on, and no complete healing had taken place yet that late into my pregnancy. My selfish prayers were only hoping to get results if they weren't in allegiance with God's plan, which made it so difficult to carry on in confidence. I felt like I was walking through the darkest valley of unknowns. Nothing felt right. Although the hospital gave me the authority to make these big decisions, spiritually, I didn't have the authority to simply choose death for someone, especially my son. But at the same time, I considered sending a life into possible torture and discomfort just as terrible. I couldn't bear pushing my son to endure a life on machines only so he can be alive just lying in his bed; it wouldn't have been fair to him. It was a hard dilemma to process.

Carston's birth would indicate all time being gone. I wanted to get it right, and God knew I didn't want to make a mistake. All things are possible with God, so then how could I have been expected to make a decision so quickly? It would have been like assuming He would do nothing between that meeting and Carston's birth, but we had already seen through our prayers that God is able. The Holy Spirit was trying to reassure me something better was planned for my son, and deep down, I could feel He was all-powerful and still able to do anything. So in the time I had left, I was in constant prayer that God would show us what to do, confident that if I asked anything according to His will, He would hear me (1 John 5:14).

I grew to pray God's version of perfection over Carston above any selfish requests I had prayed before. I wanted to be sure I was praying through God's eyes every night in petition for His direction, as though I was in Heaven looking down on my situation. I specifically asked God to move Carston from the breech to the birthing position and for a safe, natural birth. I called out miracles for his breathing and a re-creation of his lung, heart, brain, and kidneys. I prayed for him to be healed because it's always God's will to heal; that's who He is. God loved us so much that He sent His Son to suffer in our place. We do not have to live on Earth in sickness and pain because Christ already took it! Scripture says,

"This was to fulfill what was spoken through the prophet
Isaiah: "He took our illnesses and bore our diseases."

MATTHEW 8:17 ESV

"Surely he took up our pain and bore our suffering, yet we considered him punished by God, stricken by him and afflicted. But he was pierced for our transgressions, he was cursed for our iniquities; the punishment that brought us peace was on him, and by his wounds we are healed."

ISAIAH 53:4–5

"He said, 'If you listen carefully to the Lord your God and do what is right in his eyes, if you pay attention to his commands and keep all his decrees, I will not bring on you any of the diseases I brought on the Egyptians, for I am the Lord, who heals you.'"

EXODUS 15:26

In the original Hebrew in Exodus 15:26, Jehovah Rapha is used, meaning, "The Lord Who Heals." Rapha: root word; to mend by stitching, to cure, heal, repair, thoroughly make whole.[2]

Through the life of Jesus Christ, we witness His power to heal all forms of sickness and disease and to cast out demons. His crucifixion, then, does not limit us only to forgiveness and eternal life but encompasses a total deliverance of all darkness that we may experience even on Earth. In the Lord's prayer, we are instructed to pray His will on Earth as it is in Heaven, where there is no hurting, no illnesses.

"Very truly I tell you, whoever believes in me
will do the works I have been doing, and they will do even
greater things than these because I'm going to the Father."

JOHN 14:12

Knowing these truths made it easy to trust in God's power, but still, I sought after more; I was desperate to hear from Him directly, to break through the negativity swirling around me. I asked for God to help me make the right decision under the pressure I would be feeling upon Carston's arrival. I refused to answer any of the doctors' questions until we saw Carston for ourselves, saw what God could do. I prayed and prayed for God to break through the statistics and allow Carston to breathe on his own once he was born. In my mind, seeing Carston's strength to simply take a breath without intervention would be the sign I was looking for—God telling me he is ready for life here. Personally, that would confirm I was to move forward in confidence, doing whatever necessary to improve his health and comfort. In return, I agreed to give God all the glory and praise for all the things He would do and has already done.

"You need to persevere so that when you have done the will
of God, you will receive what he has promised."

HEBREWS 10:36

My Compass

I will never forget the night I woke up drenched from the waist down; the fluid wouldn't stop coming, so I jumped in the tub and yelled for Justin. I was frantic. My water broke, and it was too early; I was only thirty-six weeks along. My phone read 1:00 a.m. when I called my sister, Kayla, to come over to stay with Trinity so Justin could rush me to Riverside.

A nurse met us by the doors with a wheelchair and sent us straight up to labor and delivery, where the doctor wasted no time examining me. She began pushing all around my belly, and as her hands felt lower, she said, "I think I feel a head."

I couldn't be more relieved to hear those words! She called in the ultrasound tech to confirm, and yes, Carston had flipped head down into the birthing position. Praise God! Three days prior, my OB had reported him being butt down, but God demolished the enemy's regime once again, proving just how powerful our prayers really are and how faithful He is to us.

Miracle #3

Carston flipped from head up to head down into the birthing position on the day I was admitted.

*"Praise the LORD, my soul, and forget not all his benefits
—who forgives all your sins and heals all your diseases
…who satisfies your desires with good things so that
your youth is renewed like the eagle's."*

PSALM 103:2–3, 5

After an hour of waiting, my contractions began slowing down, so I walked the halls to progress labor on my own. I walked and walked all day until my legs were numb, but nothing at all helped, and the day was over. I settled into the unknown and couldn't help but wonder what God was doing? Justin was on the couch and Trinity in the Pack 'N Play®, resting without a care in the world, which allowed peace to rise within me. Being together was really wonderful. Anticipating God's gift quickened our hearts, strengthened our faith, and would make us a family of four, the Fearless Four.

I felt the greatest empowerment over the enemy as I chose peace in the waiting for what was next. Blocking out every negative thought that was trying to destroy me and replacing it with a worship song became a daily thing. Praise is something that terrifies the enemy and sets us free of all anxiety and worry.

*"About midnight Paul and Silas were praying and singing
hymns to God, and the other prisoners were listening to them.
Suddenly there was such a violent earthquake that
the foundations of the prison were shaken.
At once all the prison doors flew open,
and everyone's chains came loose."*

ACTS 16:25–26

Prayer and paise had broken the chains, and I had no time for chains. Praying God's will and praising His Name were the keys to letting the Holy Spirit supersede my way of analyzing everything. I was convinced this was the only way God brought me through the unknowns with an overflow of peace.

Embracing my baby would have been the best way to start the next day, but my contractions came to a total stop. I thought an induction was coming, but I was so relieved the doctor approved my request to wait and attempt a natural birth. I continued to walk the halls, ordered room service, and believed in my God's timing. Ironically enough, we already had an ultrasound and heart echo scheduled for that day, along with the determination of my C-section, so we went ahead and got those done.

What the cardiologist found in the heart echo was unbelievable! There was still a hole between the bottom chambers, including a double outlet right ventricle, but the left bottom chamber of Carston's heart fully grew to normal size, which would result in a much stronger and more manageable heart that no longer needed heart surgery right after birth!

Miracle #4

The fourth chamber of Carston's heart grew to normal size instead of shrinking as predicted.

"The blind receive sight, the lame walk, those who have leprosy are cleansed, the deaf hear, the dead are raised, and the good news is proclaimed to the poor."

MATTHEW 11:5

I was so elated about that news and couldn't wait to tell everyone, especially my doctor, but before I could say anything, she came into the room and began congratulating me on her own. That wasn't the doctor I met over a month ago; I'm certain my faith sparked something new within her. I couldn't stop praising God for re-creating the once broken yet vital organ for life!

I felt so content, but with no contractions, I received orders to pack up my things and move to the high-risk unit. Clearly, no one knew the plan besides God, and I simply had to rest in that. I gave none of the distractions that would typically frustrate me any of my devotion. I chose to search for the positive and meditate on God's purpose for me being there instead. I mean, without the setback of my labor slowing, we would have never witnessed the game-changing growth of Carston's heart, which allowed the doctors to make adjustments to their post-birth plans, leaving both them and myself encouraged for the days to come. What a great and mighty healing God we have, a God with perfect timing!

At 6:00 a.m., I was suddenly awakened by a team of nurses flipping on the lights and barging into my room. My initial thought was, "Didn't they know my two-year-old was sleeping?" I soon realized things were more serious than I could imagine. Without saying anything, they turned me on my side and placed an oxygen mask on my face. They were frantically discussing things amongst one another, and no one would answer my questions about what was going on until finally, one nurse spoke up and explained that Carston's heart was decelerating substantially. He could have been lying on his umbilical cord cutting off oxygen, or his body was signaling distress and wanting out.

I kept my eye on the monitor, along with the nurses surrounding my bed, and within seconds his heart rate starting to rise. Everyone seemed at ease except one nurse, who insisted against the other nurses that she insert an internal fetal monitor to record a more accurate heartbeat until birth. At the moment, I had no idea what this instrument was, and no one bothered to explain it to me, but luckily she couldn't find the right spot on his head to use it after all her attempts. If I knew that device screwed into my baby's head, I would have told her to get the heck out of there! God knew I wouldn't have been okay with that.

I found myself at a crossroads trying to figure out what God wanted me to do, being faced with medications I never expected. The many natural labor inductions seemed to get us nowhere. Both Pitocin® and the epidural could have lowered Carston's heartrate again, and with Carston already having a heart defect, my doctors explained that he was at an even higher risk of these drugs causing issues, which could lead to an emergency C-section, or in a rare case, death for my son. I could see frustration rising on the faces of those taking care of me as I couldn't give an answer on how to proceed.

I spent some time seeking God for clarity and rethinking the things He had already done. I sought His will with everything I had and knew He would show me which path to take (Proverbs 3:6). I felt like God must have healed Carston's heart, knowing these major events were about to come, and He had prepared him with greater strength to endure. Through God's power, Carston was already defying the odds, wasn't he? At that moment, I just knew that God already had a plan in place and was pointing to the fact that Carston would be safe. I trusted my God, the compass who leads me when I can't see clearly, so that evening I decided to move things forward with Pitocin® on the lowest dose.

Saturday, September 3, 2016

17 hours of labor

Why the Pitocin wasn't working I couldn't figure out; I was mentally, physically, and emotionally drained. My nurse increased the Pitocin every hour until I couldn't handle any more. I was in the most pain of my life, entirely depleted and still not progressing. After a night full of painful contractions and my own efforts to get Carston moving, my cervix hadn't budged at all, staying only 1.5 cm dilated.

My doctor became concerned that being on Pitocin for so long could damage my electrolytes, so she suggested an epidural as an option to get me relaxed, allowing my body to properly contract. She went on to explain a possible side effect of the epidural that it could actually bring about the opposite outcome, slowing my labor instead of speeding things up, especially if I receive it too early. She always recommends waiting until the patient is at least 3 cm dilated, but in my case, she insisted I take the risk.

The odds are never in my favor! Feeling torn and overwhelmed, there was simply no good choice to be made. I took a moment alone in my bathroom, just me, my pain, and my saving God; I really needed Him to come to my rescue. I had no clarity until Justin came in convincing me the epidural was the right thing to do. Once I was at peace with my decision, the relief couldn't come fast enough and exhaustion hit me all over again like a ton of bricks. I was in another world not even sure what was going on around me. All I knew was I wanted the pain to stop. I tossed and turned and begged for my nurse to keep checking to see what was taking so long. Finally, three hours later, the anesthesiologist arrived!

After 15 hours of low-dose Pitocin, at 9:00 a.m., I received the best shot in the world, which plunged me into a two-hour nap. The doctor came in to check my cervix, and shockingly said, "Here we go. It's time to have a baby!" They rushed me to the OR to deliver, taking every precaution and preparation for intubation, which they were fully expecting, but instead of uncertainty, I felt for the first time a spiritual confirmation that Carston would in fact breathe on his own. I've been praying and praying that if he did, it would be our signal to move forward. It was time to see the physical wonder before my eyes.

The OR was freezing cold, bright, uninviting, and crowded with nurses and residents who encouraged me to push after only seconds of being wheeled in, and there he was! Welcome to the world Carston! Weighing 4 lbs., 3 oz., 18 inches long! And oh yeah, he was breathing!

Miracles #5 & #6

#5: *Carston survived birth*
#6: *He breathed on his own without intubation*

His first breaths were very shallow, and somehow, after being bagged for a couple minutes, the doctor couldn't stabilize Carston and asked Justin if he had our permission to intubate. Justin came over to ask me, and all I could say was pray, and by time he went back to Carston, he was breathing better already on his own, so no need to intubate! Praise the Lord Jesus, all my prayers are answered:

1. For Carston to flip around and no need for a C-section.

2. For his heart grow to normal size.

3. For God to give Carston's heart immense strength through intense medications and contractions, to beat all medical odds.

4. To be born alive and able to breathe without intubation.

God's Word says, "If you abide in me, and my words abide in you, ask whatever you wish, and it will be done for you" (John 15:7 ESV). I was living proof of the very real promise in this verse. I allowed God to consume every part of me, so much so that He granted my heart's desires, which aligned with His. This bond with God grew even stronger than I ever imagined in the next moments to come with my son, as the Holy Spirit urged us to take crucial steps in preparation for the greatest war of my life.

ARTILLERY VAULT

Keep these verses at the ready for when you need strength and resolve to believe.

➤——➤ LUKE 22:42–43

➤——➤ PSALM 91:11–14

➤——➤ ROMANS 8:31

➤——➤ MATTHEW 6:6

➤——➤ 1 JOHN 5:14

➤——➤ ISAIAH 53:4–5

➤——➤ MATTHEW 8:17

➤——➤ EXODUS 15:26

➤——➤ JOHN 14:12

➤——➤ HEBREWS 10:36

➤——➤ PSALM 103:2–3, 5

➤——➤ ACTS 16:25–26

➤——➤ MATTHEW 11:5

➤——➤ JOHN 15:7

➤——➤ 1 CORINTHIANS 2:11

FAITH CHECKPOINT

*Search your heart and fortify the walls of your faith to
ensure security through the terrain of the unknown.*

*"The Spirit searches all things, even the deep things of God. For who
knows a person's thoughts except their own spirit within them? In the
same way no one knows the thoughts of God except the Spirit of God."*

1 CORINTHIANS 2:11

Praying the Will of God

Praying God's will means aligning your heart with His, through His Scripture, which is pure truth, and supernaturally, through the Holy Spirit. The Holy Spirit and the scriptures help us discern God's will because they reveal His heart and wisdom. Praying through Scripture and through the Holy Spirit provides a stronger force that fights beyond the physical things we see and can comprehend. This kind of prayer delivers greater things than we could ever come up with by our own limited requests on how things should be.

The Bible supplies us with several promises to direct us to God's will. What is the season you're walking in right now? What verses can you quote back to God in your prayer life to reaffirm your stance in truth to stay abiding in Him? Here are some that have really helped me:

He desires peace for us from the rest of the world. (John 16:33)

He will turn back our enemies from us. (Psalm 40:14)

He wants to overcome any spirit of fear within us. (2 Timothy 1:7)

He gives us the power to tread on the devil. (Luke 10:19)

He will complete what He started. (Philippians 1:6)

He hears our prayer, sees our tears, and heals us. (2 Kings 20:5)

When I pray God's will, it brings me immediate peace, although sometimes it can take long periods of prayer, praise, and fasting to accomplish the desires of His heart. If you haven't yet felt a breakthrough in your prayer time and need greater certainty, don't hesitate to ask God for a sign that could be something you physically witness or internally feel. Don't let the enemy fool you; waiting to hear God's voice is an option just as real and more beneficial as the many ideas and desires revolving in your mind. As you seek out His will, rank up in faith and remember:

- Selfish prayers only hope to get results; ask according to God's will, and He hears us every time.

- Empowerment over the enemy is electing for peace in the waiting for God's direction.

- Praying His will is a stronger force that fights beyond the physical things we see and desire.

WEAPONS OF TRUTH

What happens when we seek God's wisdom and will?

Look up the following verses in your Bible and write down what they say. Spend a moment thinking about what each verse says about *a heart that seeks after God's heart and will,* specifically. How will you respond to these truths today? Write it down.

PROVERBS 2:3–6

_____

_____

_____

_____

_____

ROMANS 8:26

_____

_____

_____

_____

_____

PHILIPPIANS 2:13

_____

_____

_____

_____

_____

HEBREWS 11:6

_____

_____

_____

_____

_____

ADDITIONAL NOTES:

_____

_____

_____

_____

_____

_____

_____

_____

CHAPTER 5

Belief Beyond Doubt

*"'But when you ask, you must believe and not doubt,
because the one who doubts is like a wave of the sea,
blown and tossed by the wind.'"*

JAMES 1:6

Y OU WOULD THINK THAT MY MEMORY OF CARSTON'S BIRTH WOULD FADE OVER TIME, BUT IT'S BEEN FOUR YEARS, AND STILL, EVERY DETAIL LIVES AT THE FOREFRONT OF MY MIND. All my gratitude, the reason I surrender everything every day, my prayer life, my influence on others, my inspiration and purpose for living, all stem from that one day my son entered the world. I remember the mother in the next room shrieking and crying like something I've never heard before. I later found out her baby was not born with a heartbeat. How is it that God chose me, chose for Carston to live?

Before I could even hold him, though, he was rushed off for further examination and testing in the NICU. Unsure about what to expect, Justin and I made it back to his little 6' x 6' room, and there he was, the tiniest baby I had ever seen, sunbathing under his heat lamp. I wanted to scoop him up in my arms, but it was impossible not to notice the CPAP mask on his face and leads stuck to his chest. He was small but mighty, crying out to us, even moving his legs when Justin tickled his toes, which was adorable.

We took pictures and enjoyed him with no distractions, nothing else going on in the world but his perfect existence. I would love to go back to those short minutes and savor them once more; I had no idea what was ahead. Once the doctor came back into the room, he told us how Carston's breathing was more stable than he ever expected, and the CPAP was precautionary. However, as he went to place a feeding tube, they found that Carston's esophagus wasn't connected to his stomach, something no one caught in the ultrasounds. He announced it so suddenly, so matter of fact, like it is what it is.

I was surprised. I really thought I would be delivering a super-healthy baby that I could just take home and testify about the rest of my life. And well, part of that is true, but God had other plans, that no matter how close I was to Him, I didn't understand. My heart sank hearing the news, but I remained strong and attentive as the doctor continued to speak. He explained that surgery would be needed if we chose to carry on with his life and that Carston would need to be transferred to Nationwide Children's Hospital to even attempt it.

I recognized his tone and felt this spirit before; I knew there was a fight ahead. The enemy would have enjoyed crushing us right then, but according to the sign God had given us, "carrying on" is what we were supposed to do, what we did do. I had to push through my distress, fully stepping into faith, with my heart, my mind, my whole being, more than ever before. I wanted God's will for Carston, and so this was a major shift in the battle where I had to stand unwavering that the greater things be done through Him. God wanted to reveal His power, and He gave us the sign to move forward. In that defining moment, it was time to rank up. This was more than Justin and I saying we believe in God's power, His presence, His plan—we were about to live it out. We decided together that moving forward with Carston's life and our decisions would be done without fear, with no room for doubt.

Even in this strong spiritual place, part of me was still very human, and there were times I wondered with new medical findings, why and how? But I couldn't stay in that place of questioning; I knew God's will and had to believe in that more than anything else. Sitting idle in doubt is the danger zone. The devil manipulates our uncertainties to paralyze us; he comes to steal, kill, and destroy (John 10:10). What begins as our own thoughts and questions, the devil twists into a trap without us even realizing it. The thief may very well be taking your growth, movement, and achievements from you. To move past doubt, source your confidence in faith and God's Word. Speak out loud with your mouth what you desire, believing you will obtain it according to the truth you know.

"So is my word that goes out from my mouth:
It will not return to me empty, but will accomplish what
I desire and achieve the purpose for which I sent it."

ISAIAH 55:11

If we are basing our boldness off of God's Word and will, then these truths will only bring the enemy a greater defeat as God performs the impossible, the unthinkable, upon our behalf.

The purpose for Carston's life became my mission. God brought us this far for a reason, and I didn't want to waver. Instead of asking God for healings and miracles, it was time I joined Him to believe the work was already done; that's why God signaled us to move forward, for His glory. Quickly getting Carston to Children's Hospital for the surgery seemed to be the best thing right then, but already I was put to the test as doctors tried to convince me that he would probably not make it through the surgery. Comfort care was brought up as still a good option, but it was not one I ever considered taking. Carston was breathing, and that was what I asked God for. I had to dig deeper than a few statistics and opinions, trusting in things that had not been done but could be done, trusting the unseen, trusting God.

"Therefore I tell you, whatever you ask for in prayer, believe that you have received it, and it will be yours."

MARK 11:24

Proof of His Power

It all came down to what I wanted for Carston, so we began preparing for the transfer to Children's Hospital. The NICU doctor covered the possibility of intubation in case Carston happened to stop breathing on the way. I stressed that I absolutely didn't want them to intubate, but ultimately, it was out of my hands, which was revealed moments later. Before they took him to the ambulance, they wheeled him into our room and over to my bedside to say goodbye, and you know, he was intubated. I should have been raging, as all of what I hoped for his independent breathing, went right out the window, but somehow I remained at peace. God's presence was all around, and I knew He was in control.

Justin rode with Carston to Children's and called me as soon as they got there. I couldn't believe what happened. Carston showed everyone he really could breathe by pulling out his breathing tube during the transport. I tried to tell them he didn't need it! God was the master of his breathing, not these machines or doctors. He was breathing room air the rest of the evening—no machines, CPAP, or extra oxygen. My boy was strong, praise God! All of this was only possible because we were obedient and believed.

At 7:00 p.m., I was still detained to my room at Riverside. I showered, ate dinner, walked, and rested, all the things I was supposed to do. I annoyingly beeped in my nurse requesting discharge papers until they finally showed up.

I was beyond ready to reunite with my son. When I finally busted through the Nationwide doors, I was rushed up to the fourth floor in my wheelchair, never more nervous or excited in my whole life. I counted the numbers above each room, 46B, 47B, 48B, then we stopped. I could hear Carston at the door, his cries sounded like a newborn kitten. I walked in amazed. There he was so innocent and sweet. He was still enjoying his heat lamp, but can you believe he was free from any breathing machine? We asked for this for Carston, and there he was; he received it, and everything was okay. He continued breathing totally on his own, even with all medical odds against him.

Carston's NICU room was a place for extremely high-risk babies who might need immediate surgery or assistance, so being right in front of the main nurse's desk gave me even greater peace of mind. Our constant nurse, Brooke, only had Carston as her assignment; no other babies or responsibilities were pulling her away. Everything seemed as perfect as it could be. Close family visited for a short time; my sister, Brittany, took an adorable video of Carston with the hiccups, and we all talked for a few minutes and even laughed a little before we said our goodbyes. The lights went down, and I wheeled the recliner next to Carston. I wanted to cradle him in my arms and snuggle with him all night, but his surgery was scheduled for the next day, and it was important he had stability in his warmer. It was hard to push aside my motherly instinct to hold him close, but with him lying in the open for me to love on so easily, I gently rubbed his face, letting him know I was there and I wasn't going to leave him.

Many doctors were in and out through the night, performing tests and examining Carston. Morning came fast, and we were already meeting with the surgeon. She got right to the point, telling us that a hole in Carston's stomach needed to be repaired before his esophagus. It really hit me out of nowhere how these findings kept coming up. I didn't say anything. I just tried to remain patient as she explained how things could actually go really wrong during and after the surgery due to his fragile state. One scenario was that if his vital signs weren't steady after fixing the hole, they would stop and not proceed with his esophagus repair. The esophageal atresia involved stretching and attaching the esophagus to the stomach, and the worst-case scenario was that Carston's heart could totally fail, unable to handle any of it, surgery or recovery. Even if the entire surgery would go well, she explained how valuable his scar tissue would be. It was the only thing that could strengthen and fully heal the esophagus. Yet, at the same time, it was also possible for his esophagus to heal tighter than normal and eventually close off, resulting in another surgery.

It was the most terrible, sick feeling, being faced with the many unknowns and not being able to physically do anything to help Carston but pick up the pen and sign him into it. Just knowing Carston would be intubated once more was hard to bear, but I knew it had to be done. Not only would he be on the ventilator for surgery, but for many days through the healing process, which could, unfortunately, allow his body to grow dependent on it, according to the surgeon.

There was no hope given and so much ahead to overcome. I would have loved even more security from God at that moment, but I knew if I had all the answers, I wouldn't need my faith. God created a mystery and gave us a choice—pursue Him even greater or rely on instincts of the flesh. I hung onto my faith because it's all I had, signing the paper to make it official. Nothing would shake my belief in a complete re-creation of Carston's esophagus and a complete restoration of Carston's stomach.

A few hours later, a team of nurses prepped him for his trip to the OR. They bundled him up and shoved a heating pad under his blanket to keep him warm. All of his monitors were disconnected and reattached to portable ones. Emergency kits and extra medical equipment stacked up underneath his mobile bed. The enemy was taunting me with the chance that something could go wrong, but I refused to accept it. There was no other option but surgery as the next step.

It took about forty-five minutes to prep Carston for transport, and before we knew it, we were off, through the hallway, into the elevator, and down to the OR. Justin and I walked with Carston all the way there. Two surgeons met us at the end of a narrow, white hallway, and the doctor said, "This is it, take one last moment with him." The air was cold, and everything around me was screaming, "This is the end!" To be honest, my physical body was shaking. I'm not sure if it was the temperature or just the fact that this felt so unreal, kissing my newborn and sending him off into what seemed like emptiness, but the assuredness inside of me overcame all of my flesh and the enemy's attempts to take me off course.

The waiting room was huge, with many couches and chairs to recline, food, and TVs. There were large monitors above the service desk, which revealed the lineup of children due for surgery. It showed the last name of the child and their status as waiting, prepping, in surgery, and recovery. Four hours went by as Carston remained in "surgery" status. I thought that if the surgery went fast, most likely something was wrong or they didn't finish, so I tried to sit contently. Finally, the receptionist called our name to inform us he was in recovery and we could see him soon.

Miracle #7

Carston made it through stomach and esophagus surgery successfully! His esophageal atresia and hole in his stomach was repaired.

"*For with God nothing shall be impossible.*"

LUKE 1:37 KJV

Sunday, September 4, 2016

I'm sitting here in total awe of my God. With surgery an astounding success, it seems like one sign after another—Carston is meant to be here with us. Everyone's praises and congratulations are lifting me even higher than I thought I could feel. Little "Captain America," some people are saying. I love it! Carston is saving the world one soul at a time through the revealed power of God!

So here I am with a superhero in my room; he actually does look completely different, swollen all over with fluid and a chest tube about the width of a pencil stemming from the surgery site out the side of his body. It's supposed to drain any excess fluid around the repair but prevents him from moving at all until he is healed. It crushes me that I haven't yet held him in my arms, but I feel good about his constant drip of morphine, that he's not in any pain.

So in the meantime, as we wait, Carston remains on the ventilator, which I hate. I've been told several times that extended use can weaken his lungs by doing most of the work for him, making it harder to breathe on his own again. All these statistics and professional opinions make it seem as if Carston has no chance of recovery and independent breathing, but I am not going to fold. I will stand on what I've already seen with my own eyes and live in this moment of expectation for more to be done, no matter what anyone says.

The surgery was the biggest giant I had yet to face. It towered over me like we didn't stand a chance. The medical facts, the possible outcomes, even death—the end of Carston's life stared me right in the face. I didn't know it then, but this intimidation would become my every day, stationed on the battlefield with countless giants that would appear out of nowhere, prepared to take me out. War came to challenge my energy, hope, belief, and point of being. Take a breath because this clear breeze of God's plan is about to get smokey as the enemy's fiery arrows released in my direction.

ARTILLERY VAULT

Keep these verses at the ready for when you need to believe beyond your doubt.

➤——➤ JAMES 1:6

➤——➤ JOHN 10:10

➤——➤ ISAIAH 55:11

➤——➤ MARK 11:24

➤——➤ LUKE 1:37

➤——➤ EPHESIANS 2:6

➤——➤ MATTHEW 6:10

FAITH CHECKPOINT

*Search your heart and fortify the walls of your faith to
ensure security through the terrain of the unknown.*

Believing Before You See

If there is one thing that will keep us from receiving a miracle, healing, or a
blessing, it's dying in doubt. It seems logical to question what we can't see,
but if we build every next thought upon a foundation of fear, the enemy will
destroy the gateway to the greater thing we are seeking. Doubt is simply the
downplay of God's power. When we ask God with doubt in our hearts, we
are limiting what we can receive, and the enemy is all over it. To open up this
passageway of God's power, we have to believe beyond our doubt, recognizing
God gave us the power over the enemy to dismiss the negative and propel us
forward, reaching what seems like the impossible.

*"And God raised us up with Christ and seated us with
him in the heavenly realms in Christ Jesus."*

EPHESIANS 2:6

When God raised Jesus, He raised us who believe as well. With Jesus as the head and us as the body, we reign over the devil and his ability to manipulate our thinking. When you are praying, take your place there next to God on the throne, declare your freedom, and bring back to Earth the victory as it is in Heaven (Matthew 6:10).

Isn't it ironic how, usually, in our weakest, most vulnerable moments, we have to stand the most firm? It's impossible to succeed when we rely on our own ability, which is already worn down and depleted. Just knowing I carry the power of God through the Holy Spirit gives me the upper hand to cast down the devil and receive through my belief. In situations where I know God's will and truth according to His Word, I no longer ask God but agree with Him that He's already done everything I need. There is no room for compromise here. Believing without doubt will produce victory, claiming faith over any mental battle or situation we face full of unknowns. What area of your prayer life can you press harder into with full belief for what seems like impossible results? As you believe in your heart without doubt, rank up in faith and remember:

- Sitting idle in doubt is the danger zone where the devil manipulates our uncertainties to paralyze us. He comes to steal, kill, and destroy. (John 10:10)

- Source your confidence in faith and God's Word. Speak out loud with your mouth what you believe to receive according to the truth you know. God's voice, God's Scripture, God's will won't return empty. (Isaiah 55:11)

- If we have all the answers, we wouldn't need faith. God created a mystery and gave us a choice. Will we pursue Him even greater or rely on instincts of the flesh?

WEAPONS OF TRUTH

What does Scripture say about why we can trust God and His power?

Look up the following verses in your Bible and write down what they say. Spend a moment thinking about what each verse says about *why we can rely on God and His power in us,* specifically. How will you respond to these truths today? Write it down.

GENESIS 28:15

_____

_____

_____

_____

_____

DEUTERONOMY 20:1

_____

_____

_____

_____

_____

MATTHEW 21:21–22

EPHESIANS 4:14–15

ADDITIONAL NOTES:

CHAPTER 6

Remember the Victory

*"'But seek His kingdom,
and these things will be given to you as well."*

LUKE 12:31

G OD SHOWS UP FOR ME TIME AND TIME AGAIN, AND AS A WITNESS AND
ACTUAL VESSEL OF HIS POWER, MY FAITH IS THE STRONGEST IT HAS
EVER BEEN. What I've seen and experienced with Carston has built my faith
tremendously. I was learning and growing through every challenge and decision made, but my boldness about God and His plan turned heads all around.
I didn't know the details about what God had in store next, but I knew it
would be good—it would be healing.

Even the surgeon came by our room, telling us how surprised she was at
how well his surgery went. Her exact words were, "It was like sewing tissue
paper together," yet the surgery was a success. She reminded us that it could
take months to heal and may never heal completely, that he was more prone to

- 97 -

contracting an infection due to Trisomy 18, which is linked to a compromised immune system and healing deficiency. She made it her point for me not to get my hopes up for a full recovery, but I simply smiled and couldn't help thinking, "My God is bigger."

And I was right. Throughout Carston's first week of recovery, Captain America shocked the world by making progress every day. He would do this thing where he held his leg straight in the air for no reason, and I couldn't help but laugh. I would push it down for him to rest, but he would get it right back up there, he was so strong. The nurse even tucked his hands under the blanket so he wouldn't pull out his breathing tube, but, of course, he worked his arms out in no time.

After six days, Carston was totally weaned from all pain meds, besides an occasional bolus of morphine when he appeared to be in pain; at least it wasn't a continuous drip. The only thing going into him was nutrients and things his body actually relied on; well, besides my milk. I pumped and pumped, only for it to be frozen and used later. Total Parenteral Nutrition (TPN) took its place for a while; it ran through a PICC line that went up his leg and into his stomach. Sadly he couldn't have a feeding tube until his esophagus was more stable, which would be checked through an esophagram about two weeks after his surgery. This procedure is performed under x-ray by sending a small tube down his throat and releasing die into his esophagus to determine if it leaks. If his esophagus is healed, his breathing tube and chest tube would be removed; but if his esophagus leaks, which they were fully expecting, he would need to rest and heal for another two weeks before they tested again.

At this point, things were looking really promising. On day seven, he weighed five pounds and was at minimal settings for breathing. Hallelujah! Carston's nurse reported his vitals as "rock solid" every morning she checked into our room. He didn't need any extra oxygen and was breathing on his own above the vent, resulting in the air pressure being lowered every day. However, concerns started to rise again as Carston's arms and legs started to shake for no apparent reason. Initially, they thought this could be a normal thing called preemie jitters, but after many days of it, they thought he could be having miniature seizures.

In my mind, there was no way I would accept yet another diagnosis to hinder my son's life. This was another jab from the enemy to provoke uncertainty about God's plan. But simply dismissing it and relying on God's power that had made a way before created results in my favor once again. A neurologist ran some tests to investigate his brain activity, which I hated because Carston had all these sticky wires on his head, but God knew what He was doing. The EEG proved communication existed on the top of the left and right side of Carson's brain where the tissue had been missing in my fetal MRI. There was officially nothing wrong with my baby's brain, and there were no seizures detected. God never stopped working on our behalf, proving the professionals and test results wrong time and time again.

"God is in the midst of her, she will not be moved;
God will help her when the morning dawns."

PSALM 46:5 ESV

One Day at a Time

When I asked God for Carston to breathe on his own as confirmation to move forward, I thought it would be easy to take the next steps, but God didn't guarantee what the days, months, and years ahead would look like. I truly planned on going home soon and enjoying life as usual, but life became anything other than what I thought it would be. Day to day, I didn't get much rest. I ran purely on adrenaline and expectation for God to move in Carston, and I could sense He was waiting for me to draw on His strength for what the day was to hold. So that's what I did; I woke up and prayed and read God's Word first before anything else. He was there with us, and I could feel Him so heavily.

*"One God and Father of all,
who is over all and through all and in all."*

EPHESIANS 4:6

My desperation disciplined me deeper into who God is and what He was saying. I relied on Him because no day was the same; there was no stability, and even though we followed a schedule for Carston's needs, the unpredictable always seemed to happen. Our everyday looked something like this, with the ups and downs of NICU life:

5:00 A.M.   CARE

Listen to heart, blood pressure, change leads, flushed his IV, suctioned his breathing tube, rotated his body, foot poked for blood labs, changed diaper and chest tube bandage.

6:00 A.M.   X-RAY

Out of his cozy warmer onto the cold board to check for tube placement.

6:30 A.M.   CHECK-UP

Once snuggled in bed, it never failed for the surgeon to arrive, unwrapping him to check stitches and chest tube. Respiratory therapist listened to his breathing, charted pressure and rate on the ventilator.

7:00 A.M.   SHIFT CHANGE

Give a full report to the next nurse taking care of Carston, including his history since birth, not my favorite, as it became the daily reminder of Trisomy 18 and all problems that came with it.

7:30 A.M.   MILK

Pumped, labeled, and stored my milk.

8:00 A.M.   ROUNDS

Carston's doctors gathered in our room, each gave an update on him according to their profession and what to expect for the day and week.

9:00 A.M.   CARE

Typical care. I changed his diaper, cleaned his mouth and eyes. He loved to suck on a Q-tip of water but absolutely hated diaper changes.

10:00 A.M.   MILK

Pumped, labeled, and stored my milk.

10:30 A.M.   MORNING ROUTINE

Couch-bed clean up, shower in locker room, praise and worship, totally exhausted but pushed through a visit from the chaplain, lactation nurse, and therapist on staff.

12:00 P.M.   LUNCH

Ate something fast in cafeteria. It was close to Carston's care. I didn't have to be present but wanted to bond in those moments with him.

1:00 P.M.   CARE

Typical care + any extra testing needed, like ultrasounds, heart echoes, EEG, and EKG's.

2:00 P.M.   MILK

Pumped, labeled, and stored my milk. I jumped online to pay bills and make needed phone calls when doing this.

3:30 P.M.   FAMILY

Trinity and Justin came to visit. We took walks, ate dinner, ran through the halls, and hugged all the animal statues.

5:00 P.M.   CARE

Typical care.

5:30 P.M.   MILK

Pumped, labeled, and stored my milk.

6:00 P.M.   DINNER

Time to separate myself and refuel unless something was wrong with Carston.

7:00 P.M.   SHIFT CHANGE

As nurse gave report, I said my goodbyes to visitors.

9:00 P.M.   CARE

Typical care + Weight. Sunday and Tuesday bath, measure length and skin team check.

8:30 P.M.   MILK

Pumped, labeled, and stored my milk.

9:00 P.M.   SLEEP

Even with the main light off, our room was still bright and noisy with constant beeping of machines and nurses in and out through the night, but I tried to get whatever sleep I could.

1:00 A.M. CARE

Typical care, but I didn't participate, instead I went to pump.

1:30 A.M. / 4:30 A.M. MILK

Pumped, labeled, and stored my milk. Totally exhausted but pushed through. It's not common for a parent to live in the NICU. I was the only one walking out in my pajamas at random times.

This schedule was nonstop, plus there were doctors who randomly met with me. I updated family and friends and visited with guests. Once Carston proved to be stable after the first few nights, his nurse gained another patient, so I helped take care of Carston more as well. It was a lot of stress, and I missed Trinity and life at home. I can't give back enough to my parents and Justin's parents who took care of Trinity, and to my close friends and family who brightened my days with positive words, gift cards, gas, money, and hot meals. In addition, the hospital's consideration of a patient's family helped us transition to this new, unstable normal, providing free parking, drinks from the cafeteria, pumping containers to store my milk, blankets and pillows for me to sleep with, plus access to their locker room for me to shower. Surrounded by help and loved ones, I still felt so heavy with this burden, growing physically and spiritually tired from the battle but persistent in the fight. It's impossible to fully put into words, for anyone to really understand what I was going through, what Carston was going through, unless you've lived it.

"The LORD is a refuge for the oppressed,
a stronghold in times of trouble."

PSALM 9:9

His Breath in Our Lungs

On day ten of Carston's life, things started getting scary out of nowhere. At 3:00 a.m. Carston's oxygen dropped to 60%, and the alarm went off to signal his nurse and nearby help. I jumped up and ran over to him; he had spit bubbles coming from his mouth, and I could clearly see his breathing tube needed to be suctioned so he could breathe again. We had to suction it quite frequently because the breathing machine put extra moisture into his lungs. On top of that, he couldn't swallow with the tube down his throat, causing saliva to build up in his mouth.

His nurse wasn't anywhere to be seen, so I ran to her other patients' room, and she wasn't there either. No one was at the main nurse's desk, and no nurses were in the hall; I was running around trying to find someone to help, then finally, a nurse walked around the corner.

I grabbed her, and by the time we got back to Carston's room, his oxygen was in the 50s, and his heart rate just as low. The nurse seemed hesitant because some patients have restrictions, but before she could even think, I frantically urged her to suction him, so she did, but it was too late for him to get his breathing up on his own. I saw the panic in her eyes as she kept looking at Carston then back at the monitor, hoping to see change. I had no idea what she was thinking, but I started yelling, "Bag him! Call someone! Do something!"

I was terrified to see everything drop without a doctor or any other help around. The nurse started bagging the hose on his vent and called for a Code Blue. Sadly, I witnessed this process many times in the NICU; the central alarm announces, "Code Blue! Code Blue!" Doctors from every direction sprint down the hall in urgency to help, but how was this happening to us? All I could think was, "Not my son! Not my son!"

It seemed like everything was crashing down, but seconds later, the manual breaths from the bag began helping Carston's oxygen and heart rate increase. Right as the team of doctors rushed in, the nurse canceled the Code Blue, and everyone just stood around him in silence, monitoring his every next breath. All his levels went right back to normal and remained steady for the following days.

I owe my life to that nurse walking in the hallway. I found out Carston's nurse was on her lunch break; she said her beeper was going off but would have never made it back in time. Another nurse was supposed to watch Carston and her other patient when she was away, but where this nurse was, I had no idea. What's crazy is after they finished helping Carston, her other patient had a Code Blue, and they all rushed in there. These nurses had multiple patients and were doing their best job, but I wondered when the last time these kiddos were checked on? Carston's first nurse, Brooke, was unable to be our primary, so there were several different nurses rotating through with Carston as we tried to figure out which one worked best with us, which couldn't come soon enough.

"They triumphed over him by the blood of the Lamb and by the word of their testimony; they did not love their lives so much as to shrink from death."

REVELATION 12:11

Coincidence Is Counterfeit

My nerves were on edge for days, where I felt like I couldn't leave Carston's room. Insecurities tried taking the place of God's voice, as the enemy would not stop preying on the unknown. Satan tried to convince me that the miracles leading up to the Code Blue were just happenstance, that Carston's healings were random and misleading. He was trying to erase my testimony, which had the power to defeat him. But as I surrendered once again, God gave me strength, and I remembered who was in control—Him, and that every battle and victory had a purpose. The silence was not God's absence; it was hope's ambiance, the opportunity for me to reflect and consider the things God had already accomplished to get me through this time. I had to set them as stone in my mind, to value and give hope for another victory to come.

After a couple of days of Carston being fully stable, things started to look bad again as he struggled to breathe. Every hour we were increasing Carston's settings, which was out of the ordinary, so the nurse called the NNP and ordered an immediate x-ray. Right away, the surgeon was notified, and her team rushed into our room within minutes. After they took a moment with Carston, they all knew something I didn't. The nurse frantically started gathering things and making calls to get him right to the OR. Then, suddenly, the surgeon stopped her and said, "This has to be done now!"

The low lights in Carston's room instantly flipped stunningly bright and became crowded with doctors in their white capes barging in, which happened more than I ever thought it would within the first two weeks of his life. The nurses came in and started prepping the surgeon and her team with proper clothes, masks, hairnets, booties, and gloves; they even taped off the room with caution tape.

I sat in shock until my nurse finally came over and explained how the x-ray revealed a large pocket of fluid built up around Carston's surgery repair site. His chest tube was clogged, and the fluid was building up inside him, desperately needing release. I remember her giving me the option to leave the room, but I insisted on staying and agreed not to get off the couch or even speak, for that matter.

Everything was swirling around me. How did this happen? How safe is this procedure? How long will it take? I wanted answers, but there was no time; the whole room was spinning out of control. To overcome the madness, I chose to let go of the concerns in front of my eyes and again reflect on what God had done and had the power to do next.

"So we do not focus on what is seen, but what is unseen.
For what is seen is temporary, but what is unseen is eternal."

2 CORINTHIANS 4:18

It took only a matter of minutes to complete the surgery, which left Carston with a larger bandage but a clear chest tube. I was thankful but also realized it would be even longer until his chest tube came out permanently, even longer until I could hold Carston. I felt like we kept taking steps forward, then another few steps back, not making much ground.

"I will remember the deeds of the Lord; yes,
I will remember your miracles of long ago."

PSALM 77:11

Preserved by Past Praise

Thankfully, Carston's chest tube remained clear, and the doctors began lowering pressure along with the oxygen on his ventilator the next morning, but rounds brought up new concerns. Carston's blood labs revealed a bilirubin level of 10 in his liver; a normal level would be zero or one. They believed it was caused by the TPN nutrition he had been relying on for the past twelve days, so they planned to place a temporary feeding tube and start weening the TPN the following Monday, along with getting his first esophagram, which was done through the same procedure. In the meantime, they decided to take one more step out of precaution and start him on a medication called Actigall®, which was supposed to help drop his bilirubin.

The blood labs also revealed a high level of creatinine in Carston's kidneys, so a urologist was scheduled to perform a dye test later that week to make sure everything was cycling normally. On top of it all, another blood lab was ordered to ensure his thyroid wasn't causing all the issues.

I'm sure I held a disturbed look on my face through that entire report; it just wasn't making sense. One doctor tried to explain that so many problems came about due to a variety of factors working against Carston. He was still recovering from surgery, trying to heal, he had to regulate all the outside material coming into his body, including the TPN nutrition, morphine, Lasix®, multiple tubes in and out, then my breast milk, along with the new Actigall® medication, which was coming next. It was a mountain of obstacles for one baby to climb, especially one with abnormal DNA who was not even supposed to be born yet. All of this led to another reassurance that ending everything, stopping all the tests and procedures was still okay if that's what I chose to do. They went on and on about the challenges, but I wouldn't let the enemy convince me to accept them; the "impossible" had already been done, the substance we once hoped for was obtained; there he was, alive and recovering, which increased my faith. Joy resides in hope, standing on past victories and anticipating new answers to come. So as I carried on through the obstacles, I held tight our victories to shut down the enemy and let faith arise.

Monday, September 20, 2016

Today I expected nothing less than a complete miracle. Yes, some complications have come up, but at the same time, many medical predictions haven't come true. Carston has continued to defeat every attempt of death the enemy has plagued on him, coming out even stronger. So, with full confidence, I remained in prayer and preparation all day today for Carston's esophagram.

The fluoroscopy room was overtaken by a huge x-ray machine. Carston was placed on the glass board, which resembled a bed underneath the overhanging device. I was handed a lead apron and ordered to stand near the doorway behind a clear dividing wall. I couldn't see what was going on or hardly contain my nerves. I waited very patiently and hope-

ful, but once the test was finished, I knew that he simply didn't pass; his esophagus wasn't healed. There were no surprised or excited expressions; in fact, no one had any care in the world, and I kept a strong face right along with them, even though I felt crushed inside.

If there is any redemption to this, it would be that Carston is finally receiving a little of my breast milk through the feeding tube, but unfortunately, this day keeps getting more unbelievable. Now Carston's heart rate is out of the ordinary, jumping up and down since we've gotten back to our room. The cardiologist just left and mentioned the possibility of SVT. I can't stop wondering why? Why, God, are these things happening? Why did their expectations come true and not the healing I was believing in?

Why do these attacks keep coming out of nowhere?

With medical concerns comes a lot of tests. Carston had to wear a twenty-four-hour monitor to record how long and how often his heart jumped around. On top of this, an endocrinologist was scheduled to run three tests on Carston's thyroid, which had little to no function, according to his blood work. The retest for his esophagram was in two weeks, but I came to know that it didn't guarantee any other issues from popping up by then. I was doing all I knew to conquer these unpredictable challenges as they came, in surrender to God, aligning with His will, believing through any doubt, and holding on to my past victories, but still, I started to get overwhelmed. It became hard to keep my head straight. I had to find a greater way to protect myself from these random attacks, not only how to endure the battle but deter the enemy and his weaponry.

ARTILLERY VAULT

Keep these verses at the ready for when you need the confidence to carry on, remembering what God has done.

➤——→ LUKE 12:31

➤——➤ PSALM 46:5

➤——➤ EPHESIANS 4:6

➤——➤ PSALM 9:9

➤——➤ REVELATION 12:11

➤——→ 2 CORINTHIANS 4:18

➤——➤ PSALM 77:11

➤——➤ JOSHUA 4:1–8

FAITH CHECKPOINT

Search your heart and fortify the walls of your faith to ensure security through the terrain of the unknown.

Memorials Build Our Confidence in God

Our faith is founded on God's truth, His Word, but even more so, our faith is built on our own personal experiences with God. Each situation where God has worked through your faith serves as a spiritual memorial, a specific memory you will never forget. If you allow it, each memorial that comes next builds your confidence in God, that He will always defend you and fight for you. The more confident we get in His ability allows us to face the unknown, not assuming our defeat but as an opportunity to press in for victory.

In Joshua 4:1–8, after the Lord miraculously stopped the Jordan River from flowing and commanded the Israelites to cross, He then told Joshua to choose twelve men, one from each tribe, to take twelve stones from the Jordan to make a memorial, to serve as a sign among them. This order was given directly from God; He orders us to make memorials. Our memorials can be visions in the spiritual realm or actual physical reminders that will not only inspire us but others if we choose to testify. I want to challenge you to bring your memorials to life by recording in a journal all the specific ways God has acknowledged you. Answered prayers, miracles, a special word from God, anything to help you stand firm when the enemy comes. Your past victories will stir up hope and empowerment over the devil. As you rank up in faith, remember:

- Trust God more than living in the moment of affliction, knowing "My God is bigger" than any impossibility.

- The silence is not God's absence; it's hope's ambiance, the opportunity to reflect and consider the things God has already accomplished to get you through.

- Joy resides in hope, standing on past victories and anticipating new answers to come.

WEAPONS OF TRUTH

What does Scripture say about remembering God and His deeds?

Look up the following verses in your Bible and write down what they say. Spend a moment thinking about what each verse says about *the power of remembering*, specifically. How will you respond to these truths today? Write it down.

JOSHUA 4:1–8

_____

_____

_____

_____

_____

PSALM 103:2

_____

_____

_____

_____

_____

LUKE 22:9

_____

_____

_____

_____

_____

COLOSSIANS 3:1–2

_____

_____

_____

_____

_____

ADDITIONAL NOTES:

_____

_____

_____

_____

_____

_____

_____

_____

_____

CHAPTER 7

"For our struggle is not against flesh and blood, but against the rulers, against the authorities, against the powers of this dark world and against the spiritual forces of evil in the heavenly realm. Therefore put on the full armor of God, so that when the day of evil comes, you may be able to stand your ground, and after you have done everything, to stand. Stand firm then, with the belt of truth buckled around your waist, with the breastplate of righteousness in place, and with your feet fitted with the readiness that comes from the gospel of peace. In addition to all this, take up the shield of faith, with which you can extinguish all the flaming arrows of the evil one. Take the helmet of salvation and the sword of the Spirit, which is the word of God. And pray in the spirit on all occasions with all kinds of prayers and requests. With this in mind be alert and always keep on praying for all the Lord's people"

 EPHESIANS 6:12–18

I HAD NO CLUE THE IMPORTANCE OF PREPARING FOR BATTLE OR HOW TO PURPOSEFULLY BE READY BEFORE THIS TRIAL WITH CARSTON'S LIFE BEGAN. I was practicing all the things Christians do, and it felt right. I was building my faith and spirit, but uncovered something even greater in the middle of this war with Carston. Every day I was enduring many challenges, more than anything life might typically bring; I faced several of what appeared to be earthly complications that were even deeper attacks against my spirit and my physical and mental wellbeing. As we are reminded in Ephesians 6:12, no matter how large or small the issue is, we have to stay aware that spiritual forces are behind it for all of us. Sometimes we don't see the attacks coming, but trust me, they will. And so the secret way of advancement in any struggle, and even before, is intentionally praying the armor of God over yourself daily so you can take your stand against Satan's schemes. In this battle of life for my son, the attacks wouldn't stop, but the armor gave me the ability to repel the enemy and hold my line when the attacks hit.

Five days went by, and Carston's bilirubin level went up to 16, making doctors concerned since Carston had been on Actigall®, along with receiving less TPN combined with my milk for over a week at this point. It was hard to believe a liver transplant was said to be a possibility for his future. I had to walk out of rounds. I went to the locker room to shower and refocus, which seemed like a good idea then, but when I was gone, Carston pulled out his breathing tube, and his oxygen immediately plummeted.

As if things couldn't get any worse that day, Carston spit up about 10mls of milk, so his nurse stopped his milk and removed his feeding tube, the one thing that could have helped naturally lower his bilirubin. Taking every precaution, he also got a stomach tube, going in through his mouth and down to his stomach to collect any more spit-up or stomach acid that could try to come out, potentially damaging his esophagus that was trying to heal. I was on the verge of losing it. Carston didn't need any more tubes, complications, or future surgeries, but I clung to the peace I had left. The battle can't eliminate our peace as long as the Holy Spirit is our core because He is Peace (Ephesians 5:22–23). The armor of God is our shell, which helped me hold it together, envisioning myself in prayer, fully covered until good news could be delivered.

As I pray the armor of God over myself, I actually apply it to my life and the current situation I'm going through. I picture fastening the belt of truth around me as I declare God's truth, His Scripture, His past victories over my situation into the atmosphere. I place on the breastplate of righteousness asking for forgiveness, because our wrongdoing separates us from God, and to be righteous, we have to repent. I strap on my sandals with the gospel of peace, praying specifically that the way is made for what God has planned that day; you know the enemy is out to do nothing less than stop anything good from happening. I take up the shield of faith, protecting my heart and spirit with the reminder that whatever is happening, God is orchestrating it all for my good. The helmet of salvation is security for my mind from the enemy's lies, that what I'm dealing with is beyond help, but Jesus died for me, which makes the way to victory possible. I carry the sword of the Spirit, which is God's Word, with me all day long, not physically, but internally, quoting Scripture and remembering stories from the Bible to inspire and direct my next steps for a win over the enemy.

Thankfully, this time my victory came with haste. The NNP reported Carston's thyroid test results as totally normal, and his heart was determined to never have been in SVT. The cardiologist concluded that his heart simply operated differently, signaling improper variability. Carston could have been on lifelong medication for his thyroid and had an even more serious problem with his heart, but my God healed, re-creating what was broken. He is always working.

Miracle #8

Carston's thyroid now worked properly, and his heart healed with no sign of SVT.

"The mind governed by the flesh is death, but the mind governed by the Spirit is life and peace."

ROMANS 8:6

"The LORD your God is in your midst; he is a warrior who can deliver,
He takes great delight in you; he renews you by his love;
he shouts for joy over you."

ZEPHANIAH 3:17, NET

A Message from Heaven

God has no limits and is always on time, knowing just what we need to carry on. His way of communicating with us to encourage a win over the enemy is just the same. I know He sent meaning to every word of this testimony I'm about to share, which empowered me to open the small box I sometimes put God in and really expand my view on how He works.

Justin's Aunt Dana came to visit and told me about her grandson Titus, who was born with Trisomy 21, also known as Down's Syndrome. Like Carston, he had several holes in his heart and could not breathe on his own. His mother, Anna, noticed at age nine months that he started having what they call head drops, where he would drop his head and jerk his eyes, then for a split second, it was like he lost consciousness, and his muscles would go limp. It was a light switch shut off, then quickly turned back on. He would have as many as thirty an hour or as little as two a day.

As a family, they would gather around Titus every night before bed and lay hands on him, anointing him with oil, and praying for him. They began to pray specifically for the head drops. At eighteen months, Titus didn't seem bothered by the frequent head drops, but Anna noticed it starting to affect his abilities. His therapist suggested he be seen by a neurologist in case these were actually seizures.

The neurologist ran several blood tests and performed an EEG, which confirmed he was having seizures and little to no normal brain activity. They started Titus on two meds that made him so lethargic he could no longer sit up to play. Another EEG was performed, and seizure activity was still prevalent, so the neurologist added two more medications that made him even more unresponsive.

Now he would go all day without opening his eyes, even while eating. He hated his food because he was so full of medicine. He stopped almost all forms of communication and eye contact. So, at twenty-five months, the neurologist then prescribed a new drug. Anna and Sven had to learn to give him injections at home every day. After forty days of this, they thought they noticed less seizure activity, but he was still on four medications and would just lie on the floor with his eyes cracked open ever so slightly. The doctor ordered another EEG to see if the injections were working, but the test still showed a lot of seizure activity.

At this point, the therapist said he had lost almost all of his gross motor skills, but still, the doctors increased his prescriptions once again. Things just seemed hopeless for Titus, but his family continued to pray and anoint him each night. After a full year of this, Sven and Anna decided on their own to wean him off the meds slowly until finally, he was on no medication. At that moment, Titus awoke! His big, beautiful brown eyes they hadn't seen in so long finally opened, and he started babbling, moving around, sitting up, and holding toys. Their lifeless boy was gone, but they noticed he still had seizures. As time went on, the seizures did not increase but remained the same, so they saw no reason to place him back on any medications since they weren't helping anyway.

At thirty-three months old, something amazing happened. One night Anna and Sven hosted a Bible study, with only Anna's parents, Dana and Don, and Anna's young children, Laila, Sophia, Titus, and Wyatt. At the end of the night, they circled up in prayer, and Don began to pray. All of a sudden, Titus burst into laughter and belly laughed for five minutes! Something they'd never seen before. Don continued to pray, and Titus just kept laughing. Sven and Dana both said they felt God was working on Titus in the midst of that prayer, and ever since that Thursday evening, Titus has not ever had another single seizure!

I was so thirsty for this kind of news, an outside reassurance of an incredible miracle in the midst of us trying everything and pushing on in faith.

Once they left, I felt a strong urge to walk up to Carston and just pray. As I began to speak over him, he grew this huge smile that I had never seen him express before. I just knew after hearing that story this was a sign. I knew Carston was healed at that moment, just the same as Titus.

"You have granted him his heart's desire and have not with-held the request of his lips. You came to greet him with rich bless-ings and placed a crown of pure gold on his head."

PSALM 21:2–3

His Glory Revealed

I woke up the next morning undeniably knowing in my spirit that Carston was healed; not even the doctors' negative predictions could budge my stance. They all determined it was a bit early for his esophagus to have enough scar tissue to provide a leak-proof seal, especially with Trisomy 18. I kept hearing that over and over again, lack of life, lack of quality, lack of ability; I didn't think they would ever stop trying to convince me to just give up. I became so tired of their attitudes, and I tried my best to hold my tongue, knowing they solely rely on science and their medical education.

So that afternoon, they ran Carston's feeding tube through his mouth and down into his first intestine instead of his stomach, hoping to prevent any spit-up. He also started a new drug called Erythromycin, which helped move milk through his intestines faster, but still, the stomach tube stayed in, continuing the collection of any extra milk that did try to come up from his intestines.

Justin called off work to be with us that day, and Amber came but stayed behind, waiting for us in Carston's room. Over in fluoroscopy, the nurses' smiles and surprised expressions were confirmations of what I already knew—Carston's esophagus was healed! I literally fell to my knees praising God, just bawling my eyes out. I told the nurses how I'd been praying about this from day two of his life, and one replied saying, "Well, God really does answer prayers, doesn't He?" Only his second esophagram, and already no leak!

◇ *Miracle #9*

Carston's esophagus was healed!
Passed esophagram within four weeks.

"…and the people all tried to touch him, because power was coming from him and healing them all."

LUKE 6:19

It's ironic how that day, September 28, was actually Carston's due date, and there he was, alive and healed. I will never forget that evening when Carston's surgeon peaked her head into our room and said, "Wow, momma, congratulations!" and I couldn't help but smile, knowing she had been full of doubt from the beginning. She made her way over to Carston to remove his chest tube and bandage him up.

The next morning, the first thing I did was hold Carston. Our nurse explained the entire process of getting him out of bed and the proper way for me to hold him. She emphasized the importance of making no sudden movements because his breathing tube was taped to my clothes and the chair and could be easily pulled out.

It was awkward getting him situated at first, but he ended up being at total peace. I just melted in the chair. I was his mother, his protector, his advocate, his comfort; I was his everything. As he rested on my chest, all the broken pieces of my heart were mended, all the struggles, sleepless nights, and tears were all worth it. It was like he was telling me, "Thank you, momma…now, let's keep kicking butt."

After holding him for almost an hour, it was time for his next care. With his chest tube gone, he could actually wear baby clothes instead of being swaddled in blankets all the time. It was hard to wrap my mind around all the things I was missing out on. I held my almost four-week-old baby, and with tears in my eyes, dressed him for the first time.

"I can do all things through him who gives me strength."

PHILIPPIANS 4:13

One Month Old

As each day went by, I was stretched further than I ever imagined I could be. I thought for sure Carston would have been home and healed already, but I tried my best to carry on with a brave face and faithful heart as God's plan unfolded.

Even with Carston's stomach tube in place, he started gagging and spitting up some sort of stomach acid. It continued for a few days as doctors tried to find a reason for this happening. They searched for an obstruction in his intestines, stopped my milk, started it back up, slowed it down, and started a new drug to reduce his stomach acid called Azithromycin®. Nothing really worked. He kept sticking his tongue out, letting us know something was bothering him.

One day I tried comforting Carston in my arms, but something even more terrible happened. I felt air coming from his mouth, and he was breathing heavier, so his nurse laid him on his bed to see what was going on, and sure enough, his breathing tube slipped out. His NNP and respiratory team were notified and rushed in to examine him. With his oxygen saturation remaining stable and unaffected, the nurse peeled the neo bar from his cheeks and pulled the tube completely out. They placed him on a nasal cannula, then right into my arms, a time I will cherish forever. I was praying and praying until, after a few minutes, his lungs were clearly working too hard to breathe on their own. To prevent his lungs from collapsing, they reintubated him.

I was devastated over the whole thing. It was my fault that the tube came out, and reintubating him had the potential to crush me. But it didn't crush me because I was dressed for battle. After my emotions settled, I was able to see a good reason for his breathing tube coming out because he stopped gagging, which told us he had developed a sensitivity to the position of the breathing tube. Nothing was physically wrong with him. It also revealed how at least for some time, Carston was able to breathe on his own. His brain gave his lungs the signal even to take a breath, which was another common concern with his T18 diagnosis. Although his lungs struggled, his heart rate and oxygen remained normal, which was a positive sign that he had the potential for a proper extubation. The doctors said more time would strengthen his lungs, so again, we waited and pressed into God. That situation could have turned out a lot worse, but God's armor is protection from problems we never see coming, and prevention of the enemy's provoking.

"And we know that in all things God works for the good of those who love him, who have been called according to his purpose."

ROMANS 8:28

If Carston hadn't just had his esophagus repaired, the doctors would have used CPAP instead of reintubating. CPAP is a mask that adds pressure into the lungs as the patient initiates their own breaths. Carston couldn't utilize this yet because the pressure could have busted open his esophagus that was so new to being healed. Most babies transition from the breathing tube to CPAP, then nasal cannula. Carston had to transition right to the nasal cannula, which is close to impossible for a full Trisomy 18 baby to do, but we knew God had a plan, and it was about to unfold for his next extubation scheduled for the following week.

"You are my refuge and my shield; I have put my hope in your word. Away from me you evildoers, that I may keep the commands of my God!"

PSALM 119:114–15

Force Out Feelings, Fight with Truth

It all started early in the morning with Carston's first care, which involved a foot prick for blood labs. His nurse had to squeeze, squeeze, and squeeze his foot; I cringed the whole time, wondering when this testing will ever end? The test came back revealing a low red blood cell count, so Carston received a blood transfusion. Once finished, the nurse swaddled him up, leaving in his IV so he wouldn't need to be pricked again if more labs were ordered.

I was exhausted from a typical long night of beeping machines and random doctors coming in charting numbers; I had to lay down for a nap. Carston also seemed at peace, so the nurse decided to leave his room to ensure we could both get some uninterrupted sleep.

After about an hour, I woke up and walked over to see Carston, and there laid a massive puddle of blood leaking from around his IV, drenching three blankets! I yelled for his nurse, who appeared just as in shock as I was. In a panic, she ordered new blood and began prepping him for a new IV. It was worrisome enough that he lost all that blood, but then on top of it, he had to be bothered again with another needle. At that point, I just couldn't take much more, and out of nowhere, I felt lightheaded like I was going to pass out. There had never been a nurse who hit his vein the first time; they all would say, "He is a hard poke." So one after another, different nurses were called in, and after multiple pokes and a mother filled with tears, the NNP finally hit a vein.

A couple of hours later, the doctors came by. One stepped into our room and said with a smile, "It's time to extubate," like nothing had ever happened. They could all sense my hesitation, and the same anxious doctor went on to convince me, "Even through the setback this morning, Carston's vitals have remained solid, so why not give it a try?"

I was not feeling confident at all, but God's timing is always a mystery. I was ready to see what He had in store for Carston. The NNP and respiratory team got everything in place, including medication to reduce any swelling in his throat that they noticed last time, then the nurse removed everything from his face. Carston loved having his mouth totally free! At first, he was breathing strong, but his lungs began to retract after only a few minutes, so we tried the nasal cannula with 100% oxygen, but that wasn't helping.

Carston's doctor consulted his surgeon for approval to try CPAP because, after all, his esophagus had proven to be healed. The surgeons were reluctant, fearing this could still be too soon, that the scar tissue may not be built up enough to withstand the pressure, but they finally gave in, agreeing it may be the only option to get him breathing on his own. The respiratory team wheeled in this much smaller machine and prepared the mask. It had soft Velcro straps that wrapped around Carston's head, holding a purple, rubber cup over his nose that forced air pressure. He absolutely hated it; he fought the whole time unless I was holding and bouncing him.

I bounced him for a good two hours until my arms were literally numb. It was about 3:00 p.m. when the doctors came back and noticed Carston working hard to breathe, which resulted in another intubation. When the nurses were prepping him, they suctioned his throat and found a small amount of blood. Not sure what the blood was from, they carried on cleaning his mouth and said they would keep an eye on it. Not to mention during the intubation, his stomach tube slipped out of his mouth, which is meant to suction any excess milk and acid from his stomach.

As if this wasn't enough, right after intubating, his IV started gushing blood! Again! Things literally couldn't get any worse. With no answers, the doctors ordered a blood lab to check his platelets because they thought his blood was not clotting. So the nurse removed his leaking IV and started poking his heel again to withdraw blood to test, ugh! Surely, we had enough blood, everywhere! Remembering these times still makes me hurt as his mom, but I can be at ease now seeing how crucial it was to set up God's power.

Still, it was impossible for me to know what I know now. I really felt numb. I thought God would see Carston's struggle and our sense of urgency for Him to come through that day. It was difficult to keep believing in something I needed for my son right then because, at the same time, I realized it could be so far away. Somehow, I had to carry on and fight this enemy with the sword of the Spirit, knowing God's thoughts are higher than my thoughts, and His ways are higher than my ways. Without Scripture aiding me, I would have been taken out right then and there. My feelings and thoughts were saying, "Just give up!" but God's Word is the blade that cuts Satan for our breakthrough, not our emotions. In fact, Satan can be the puppeteer of our emotions to trigger acts that aid our downfall. It's okay to feel, but match it up with God's truth before you take the next step.

Once Carston's blood filled the tube, it almost instantly clotted, which told the doctors he didn't have a platelet problem, praise God. With little time to process everything, we traveled downstairs to fluoroscopy to get his stomach tube placed back in. Unfortunately, it was our second most visited room of the hospital. Carston had two tubes in his mouth—the stomach tube catching excess acid and milk and the breathing tube, plus his feeding tube still down his nose and into his first intestine, which had to be irritating. The nurse gave him a bolus of morphine to calm down and help ease any of his pain.

The doctors planned to extubate again in two weeks. Until then, they were planning to make changes to Carston's food and digestion, as they called it his "feeds." They planned to change to full breast milk going straight to his intestines, meaning no more TPN! If everything went well, his feeding tube was going to be pulled back into his stomach and his stomach tube removed, with hope the milk would move in the right direction, having no spit-ups. I couldn't ask for enough prayers this season—for Carston, for myself, my family. I even prayed for everyone praying for me, that they would keep believing and hanging in there with me when it looked so dark. I couldn't have done this battle alone.

Tuesday, October 11, 2016

Dear God,

Thank you for all you have done. Thank you for fighting for me and sustaining me. Please, God, help me; my body is resting but my mind will not stop. I feel so terrible for Carston. I want you to take away all this torture. It's near impossible to seeing him in pain and handling these setbacks. I know the problem is not the procedures or the doctors, but the enemy and his plot against my son's life. So I pray that Carston and I can both stand firm with everything you've given us to fight this battle. You've shown me that Carston can breathe, that he will breathe without this machine, so I press forward secure with this truth, nothing will stop us. Forgive me, Lord, for any doubt that could have hindered us thus far.

Continue to make a way, guiding and directing me to accomplish Your will. I know regardless of any outcome, no matter how bad it looks, as long as I follow You, it will benefit my life. You've taken it all on the cross already—sickness, sadness, confusion; I surrender my whole self to you as you have claimed our victory here. I am confident, God, that you will carry this work to completion. You are re-creating Carston and strengthening him in this very moment for something even more triumphant to take place. I ask these things for Your glory to be revealed through my son's life, and I give You the upmost praise.

In Jesus' Name, Amen.

ARTILLERY VAULT

Keep these verses at the ready for when you've done all you can do to stand and need reinforcement with God's protection and provision.

➤——➤ EPHESIANS 6:12–18

➤——➤ EPHESIANS 5:22–23

➤——➤ ROMANS 8:6

➤——➤ ZEPHANIAH 3:17

➤——➤ PSALM 21:2–3

➤——➤ LUKE 6:19

➤——➤ PHILIPPIANS 4:13

➤——➤ ROMANS 8:28

➤——➤ PSALM 119:114–15

➤——➤ 2 CORINTHIANS 2:11

FAITH CHECKPOINT

*Search your heart and fortify the walls of your faith to
ensure security through the terrain of the unknown.*

Pray on the Armor of God

Spiritual warfare is as real as everyday life playing out in front of you, and
we have to believe that truth with all our might before we can even engage
in combat. The enemy's first trick is to strike us with unbelief; he wants to
deceive us so badly, to believe that nothing is happening because we can't see
it, so we don't fight him. The truth is, though, Satan is always after us, and
he uses the people and situations in our life as pawns in his game of destruc-
tion. So it's not even the person you're having conflict with that's the problem;
it's the enemy using them to get to you. Instead of growing angry at people
and problems that arise in life, take it out on the master manipulator behind
it all. Second Corinthians 2:11 tells us that we are not to be unaware of the
devil's schemes. We know he uses arrows of unbelief, deception, distraction,
shame, guilt, and pride, and we can combat his attacks with each piece of
God's armor, preventing these weapons from ever piercing us. Consider what
God's artillery could do for your spiritual, emotional, and mental wellbeing,
then take a step further and engage in combat by actually praying it through.
As you rank up in faith, remember:

- The battle doesn't eliminate peace. The Holy Spirit is our core,
  and the armor is our shell.

- God's armor is protection from problems we never see coming,
  and prevention of the enemy's provoking. "And we know that
  in all things God works for the good of those who love him,
  who have been called according to his purpose." (Romans
  8:28)

- God's Word, not our emotions, is the blade that cuts Satan for
  our breakthrough.

WEAPONS OF TRUTH

*What does Scripture say about our enemy and
how to protect ourselves against him?*

Look up the following verses in your Bible and write down what they say. Spend a moment thinking about what each verse says about *how Satan works, and how we should respond,* specifically. How will you respond to these truths today? Write it down.

PROVERBS 16:18

_____

_____

_____

_____

_____

JOHN 8:44

_____

_____

_____

_____

_____

2 CORINTHIANS 2:10–11; 11:3

_____

_____

_____

_____

_____

1 PETER 5:8–9

_____

_____

_____

_____

_____

ADDITIONAL NOTES:

_____

_____

_____

_____

_____

_____

_____

_____

_____

CHAPTER 8

Strength in the Waiting

*"'I have given you the authority to trample on snakes and scorpions
and to overcome all the power of the enemy;
nothing will harm you."*

LUKE 10:19

CARSTON FINALLY ACCEPTED A CONTINUOUS DRIP OF MY MILK AND WAS DOING GREAT FOR TWO DAYS IN A ROW, BUT THEN OUT OF NOWHERE HIS HEART RATE AND OXYGEN LEVEL RANDOMLY DROPPED DOWN INTO THE 70s. They even bagged him to bring him out of it a couple of times. His testing came back indicating an infection contracted from the pic line used for his TPN nutrition. He didn't need this tube anymore, yet it was still in his body. I was livid. I wanted someone to blame, and I wanted more progress. I was desperate to be free from the madness, desperate for Carston to be free! But freedom wouldn't ring for a while. They put Carston on antibiotics, and they tested his blood day after day to detect the level of bacteria. His next extubation was put on hold.

The battle was ever-changing, and this was a time where the pressure surrounding me became near unbearable. I kept thinking of the once-normal life I had outside of Carston's tiny room. I missed the joy of raising Trinity and hated the feeling of abandoning her. I so desperately yearned for the peace of home and had no bed or quiet place there at the hospital. Although Justin tried never to complain, I remember seeing the fatigue in his eyes. He was overwhelmed between work, spending time at the hospital and his parents' house, and running extra errands. It was my dream to leave the hospital as a whole family, attend church again as a family of four, and for Carston to be healed and our family complete. Still, I wondered how much longer I could take, trying to survive in the chaotic atmosphere.

It was hard to face the doctors each day Carston struggled with his staph infection and low resting heart rate that would rise no greater than 70. The doctors ordered an EKG and heart echo, which showed his heart in an abnormal rhythm called a junctional heartrate, meaning his chambers were pumping abnormally, and his electrical activity showed ischemia. He was just lying there, limp, fully relying on the ventilator to breathe, as doctors were in and out preparing us for his death. I was stunned by the way they were talking. I never asked for opinions, but they always gave their predictions, full of facts and impossibilities. The cardiologist, NNP, attending physician, and several nurses all told me this is what they typically see before a baby passes away, an overall weak system with a heart that will beat slower every day until it doesn't beat at all. Everything they said, I'm sure, is true, but I tried to block it all out. I refused to claim death but instead a re-creation of his blood and internal organs. I knew Carston wasn't finished yet on this earth, and I kept reminding myself to walk by faith, not by sight (2 Corinthians 5:7).

After an incredibly trying five days of the bacteria roaming in his system, his test finally came back negative for staph. Only through God's power, his heart rate began to rise back into the 130s, and we actually lowered settings on his breathing machine that same day. He was growing stronger into life, not weaker in death as the hospital claimed him to be. I respect the many professionals' expertise, but there's absolutely nothing man can predict within a situation controlled by God!

Miracle #10

Carston defeated death as God healed his staph infection.

"Now the Lord is the Spirit,
and where the Spirit of the Lord is,
there is freedom!"

2 CORINTHIANS 3:17

I was truly happy that so many advances were taking place for my son. With everyone noticing Carston's strength and perseverance to live, they gave us orders to move rooms. I loved our big room, but it was for babies who needed more care, emergency surgeries, extra monitoring, and extra space for crowds of doctors. It was time to move on, to move forward, and I was so ready. My son was said to be fragile but was strong, proclaimed broken and unable to heal, but re-created through Christ, and we were breaking the barriers to make it known.

Has there ever been negativity spoken over you? Doubt that you can't achieve a goal? Lies about who you are? What about a generational curse, like addiction, abuse, depression, even a physical diagnosis? Through our tongues, we hold the power to speak life and death (Proverbs 18:21); in fact, this very world was spoken into existence (Genesis 1:3). I want to encourage you to use your voice full of faith to cut off any hold the enemy has over you as he tries to substitute his false claims with biblical truth. Without works, our faith is a dead faith (James 2:26), so live out your freedom by pushing through what used to be your boundary because everything you want is on the other side of obedience.

We physically broke that barrier for Carston as we unlocked the wheels to his bed and rolled him three rooms over to the "cubby," a small section of four rooms divided from the hallway with double doors. We went all the way to the back corner room with a large window overlooking the hospital. Although smaller, it was quieter, so no more phone calls and beeping noises from the nurse's desk, no one walking past our room searching for another patient. It was a little more private and quaint.

Along with our room change, a new nurse took over that day. She walked in the room as if she owned it and handled Carston like she had known him since birth. I had seen her before with other patients, just walking through the halls, noticing her strong, enthusiastic personality, African accent, and various braided hair-do's. I thought it was neat to have the opportunity to live our days there with her. Before I got to say much at all, she said with no hesitation, "I'm Laila, and I'm available to be your primary nurse if you would like that?" I could tell Laila had many years of experience, undoubtedly confident in what she was doing, so I didn't hesitate to accept her right away as Carston's new primary. No one ever offered Carston a new bed, but one of the first things Laila did was change him over from his warmer to an actual crib with rails that went up and down. We went big, changing rooms, beds, and nurses all in one day. I was so glad to have Laila and a new outlook on the way things were done in the NICU.

Carston loved watching his mobile go round and looking at himself in the mirror. At seven weeks, he weighed 5 lbs., 3 oz., and was gaining weight consistently. After some debate, the doctors finally removed Carston's stomach tube; I was ecstatic. One less tube in Carston's body! On my request, they also pulled his feeding tube back into his stomach instead of placing a permanent OG tube into the intestines. The doctors weren't sure if his stomach would ever fully function due to the hole that was repaired, along with his underlying Trisomy 18, but this was a huge leap forward as his stomach processed my milk in the right direction. I had so many goals and desires for him; I couldn't wait to feed him by mouth and care for him without those circumstances. We weren't going to just settle for what was easy; we were expecting Carston fully healed! I was thankful our team was finally listening. On top of this, Carston's bilirubin was finally all the way down to a 1, meaning his liver was just fine! Praise God!

Miracle #11

Carston's liver was fully functional. Bilirubin at 16 down to a 1.

*"I sought the LORD and he answered me;
and delivered me from all my fears."*

PSALM 34:4

God's Strategy in Disguise

After ten days of Carston improving from his infection, the enemy couldn't stand my joy, and he tried to throw me off with another scare of SVT, where Carston's heart rate jumped into the high 200s out of nowhere. Amazingly enough, cardiology found that the lead was double-counting, so when Carston's rate was a 130, the machine read 260. *Carston had never been in SVT!* In preparation for his next extubation, a final heart echo and EKG proved his healing but revealed that Carston's heart was pumping too much blood to the lungs and was working a little harder than normal, issues that correlated back to the heart problem he was born with, double outlet right ventricle. It didn't sound good, but somehow giving him Lasix® was a simple fix until his heart surgery, which was still a possibility for the future. Lasix® pulled fluid from his lungs and actually aided his breathing even better, preparing him for his next extubation.

This was the last time they planned to extubate Carston. There had been a total of five extubations at that point, whether through a doctor's attempt or an accidental pulling of the tube. Too many times of the tube going in and out could have caused further complications and damage. They told me his lungs were strong enough, his repair sites were healed, and his heart rate remained stable, so they thought there wasn't a reason why he wouldn't be able to breathe on his own if he was ever going to. I was so encouraged by everything the doctors put in place, and I knew Carston would breathe again.

It's what God confirmed to me at his birth, so there was no room for fear. I thought, *This has to be it!*

"We are hard pressed on every side, but not crushed; perplexed, but not in despair; persecuted, but not abandoned; struck down, but not destroyed."

2 CORINTHIANS 4:8–9

In full belief Carston would come off the ventilator, I covered him in prayer that morning, along with his room and his doctors. I was jittery all over, nervous but ultimately excited for what was to come. Medically the doctors did everything they could to give him the best chance to breathe; they gave him a steroid to reduce inflammation in his airway, and his feeding tube was moved from his nose into his mouth. When the breathing tube was pulled out, they immediately placed the CPAP mask on him with the highest setting of CiPAP, which gave Carston an extra breath and pressure into his lungs, even when he didn't initiate it.

I felt at ease when one by one, each doctor left the room, confident in Carston's stability. The most wonderful thing about the CPAP machine was I could actually reach in and grab Carston out of his crib myself. The joy in little things brought me great humbling that I can't help but carry with me even today as I lift my baby girl "Laila" out of her crib, in her own room, without any machines. It is a true honor and blessing many moms take for granted.

Everything was perfect until a few hours in, when Carston worked his feeding tube right out of his mouth. He was on continuous feeds, which made this a big problem because my milk was dripping everywhere! A few calls were made after the nurse cleaned up, and we took him down to fluoroscopy to get a new one placed. Ugh, it was so aggravating. He did just fine with the procedure initially, but things started to go downhill from there. As his oxygen saturation dropped, the doctors increased his oxygen on the machine hour by hour until gradually we gave him 95% oxygen, yet the saturation in his lungs read only 70%. His heart rate was great, but it was obvious he struggled to keep breathing. After nine hours, the doctor said his lungs sounded partially collapsed, and we reintubated.

My heart plummeted. I was totally devastated and numb. The battlefield was messy, and slaying the enemy for my son's life was never easy. With a lack of understanding, confusion struck me, making me wonder, "Why wouldn't God help him through this?" Carston was medicated and fast asleep, but I grabbed my bags and kissed him goodbye with tears flowing. I felt incredible guilt for walking away after living in the NICU for two months not missing a moment with Carston, but I wasn't okay. I just couldn't take much more. I was hysterical and sick to my stomach. I was at my weakest point in this war for my son's life, running on faith and adrenaline. I was all over-exhausted, physically and spiritually, but making no ground. For the first time, I couldn't focus on God, and my feelings were taking over. It would have become toxic if I didn't separate myself from the enemy's lies. If I was going to fight this battle, it was clear I had to hold a higher stature, walking in a manner worthy of the call I was assigned. God called me back home to gain clarity and rest, to meditate in His presence, suit up with new armor, then once again charge the battlefield with His sword in hand.

Maybe you've been there before—angry, exhausted, overwhelmed with emotions, and not sure how to carry on next in our battle, if you can even carry on. Remember, these initial feelings do not mean defeat. To keep going, don't forget the drive in the middle of your weakness. It's not the emotions that carry our ability; it's the core of why we're doing what we're doing. Take time to rest and gain strength and spiritual clarity for your fight. As for me, I had to physically separate myself from the distractions and felt led by the Holy Spirit to start fasting. In Daniel 10:2–14, God noticed Daniel fasting. He knew his heart and, in return, sent Daniel an angel to give him a revelation. That's exactly what I needed here, a better understanding of what was going on. Through the crucifixion, the price was paid for Carston's freedom to breathe, so why yet haven't we received it? I decided to press in closer to God by stripping away my desires, giving up whatever it took to carry on in the security of Christ to break the bondage over my son.

With a reset mind of discipline and reliance upon God, I was ready to face the music at rounds the following day. The doctors reiterated how the longer

Carston was on the breathing machine, the more prone his lungs were to infection and dependency upon the ventilator, which I heard all the time. All the extubation attempts had failed, whether it was scheduled or Carston pulling it out on his own; he couldn't do it. They shared that the only other option to get him off the ventilator was to trach him; however, none of the doctors would actually agree with it being done because of the many other issues he had, creating impossible odds of surviving the surgery. His attending physician said she didn't think a doctor in the whole country would recommend tracheostomy for him, so that quickly got thrown off the table. However, they didn't hesitate in telling me comfort care was still an option, that there was nothing wrong with letting him pass away peacefully in my arms. They were trying to console me the only way they knew how, to encourage ending things plain and simple, which meant all the complications and stress would be over. One doctor literally said that.

The enemy never seemed to stop fighting me for my son. I couldn't imagine saying goodbye to Carston's beautiful face, but at the same time, I knew that pushing him further into a life of obstacles and mountains we would never be able to overcome wouldn't have been fair either. They were valid points, but I didn't let myself get sucked into that mind game the enemy tried on me constantly. In my spirit, I felt that bigger things were coming, and the only way to explain this was that God filled my mouth with the words to convince the doctors to give him one more try, one final extubation.

Even though I got my way, the odds were greatly against us. For the days following, there were many people in and out preparing me for the extubation to fail. From most nurses, doctors, and even counselors, I heard about comfort care on a daily basis. I tried so hard to stay encouraged and bring joy to Carston's room in the midst of doctors trying to use medical facts and terminology to persuade my thinking that breathing for Carston was impossible and quality of life for him also impossible. Although it's their job to educate parents on their child's condition, I already knew his diagnosis and every new milestone or setback he had each day on top of it. They knew I was there every day, all day. I asked questions, and they gave me answers, yet they still pushed with their comments and opinions. They assumed because I was young, I was also naïve, with no regard for their medical knowledge. To them, trusting in my God meant nothing; it meant weakness if anything; it's wasn't tangible, you couldn't predict it, and you couldn't guarantee it.

My frustration was building, but I held my composure every time, remaining polite in telling them I was still choosing to carry on. They knew of my faith and desires, so I stayed short with them; all the talk about death had to stop! The only thing I would have regretted is making that final call to pull the tube knowing he wouldn't breathe, knowing I would be causing him to purposely suffocate and die, ending his life and God's plan for it. I just couldn't live with that. I hated these moments where Carston wasn't advancing, but he was happy and bright-eyed unless he had a poopy diaper or some sort of test done; then, he cried just like any other baby. He moved his head and eyes to our voice; he moved his whole body, arms, legs, hands, and feet, especially when Justin tickled them. He did a long blink, which I called winking, with his eyes, and he sucked on his tubes. There was hope for his future, but as Laila explained to me, the doctors could only see their paperwork, and the bottom line was that paper read "Trisomy 18," where only 10% of those babies make it to their first birthday. The doctors' job was to focus on the problem and fix it, but Carston's case was much more complicated, with obstacles they thought he would never overcome. They couldn't tell me that Carston would have "quality of life," as they referred to it; they just kept pushing and pushing with their statistics.

My brain was so full that the only way to release it was also to release my flesh and step deeper into God's presence. I desired more of Him and less of myself, believing without a doubt Carston could breathe, believing God would break the chains keeping Carston bound. I fasted and prayed specifically for his lungs to be strong and for the tube not to slip out or any other issues to come up before then. I prayed for God's will to be done in his life and felt reassurance this had to be part of it. I remembered the sign I had asked for weeks before Carston was born, and with that, God knew I didn't want to rely on machines for him to live. God signaled us to move forward; He always keeps His promises and is dedicated to complete His work. I was ready for Him to reveal His power to these doctors, which I knew was the only way Carston would overcome.

"Jesus looked at them and said,
'With man this is impossible, but with God
all things are possible.'"

MATTHEW 19:26

Every Possibility Eliminated

I hardly got any sleep the night before Carston's extubation. The anticipation was building to see God's hand move in mighty ways. Carston stayed rested and at peace that night; no alarms went off, and nothing strange happened. That made it so much easier to rise with a smile and start the day with worship and prayer. It was clear that God doesn't work on anyone's timeline but His own; however, it was still my responsibility to pull Carston's healing down from the courts of Heaven as I waited. I was confident but growing anxious, waiting and pacing around his room. There was so much pressure and expectation for Carston and for God to move big.

The NNP, attending physician, respiratory therapist, and many nurses showed up to get things situated. In preparation to pull the tube, six different doctors surrounded Carston's bed and watched the monitors. They brought emergency boxes into the room and the CPAP machine soon after. The CPAP mask was ready to be placed on him directly after they took the tube out, which would be on the setting of CiPAP again, giving him the best chance to breathe with less work for him to do in the beginning.

As the doctor pulled out the tube, I was praying and standing firm in his healing. Carston remained totally calm until the respiratory therapist, an older lady who was very rough looking, forced the mask on him. She was moving his head around, pulling the mask all over. I wanted to say, "Hang on a minute, be more gentle!" but I didn't. I knew she was trying to be quick, getting everything accurately placed and secure. Carston continued thrashing his head all around, and the mask never moved. After about two minutes of watching the monitors, the doctors felt he was stable and left the room.

Once I was situated in the recliner, Laila helped me get Carston out of bed so I could hold him. I remembered from the last extubation, the only thing that calmed him was bouncing him on my lap, so again that's what I did. An hour went by, and his attending physician stepped in. She listened to his lungs and said everything sounded good, which didn't surprise me, as we were only an hour in, and if God was going to do this, only time would tell.

My mom called to check in, asking if she could come to see Carston and help out once she got off work at 2:30 p.m. The timing was perfect because I had bounced Carston for over two hours and my arms were literally numb. Many doctors were in and out checking on Carston, and nurses who knew him peeked their heads in for a quick glance at his monitors, cheering him on.

Everything was perfect, at almost 8:00 p.m. I grew nervous as the nine-hour mark was nearing, which was usually Carston's breaking point. I remember being shaky, I was sure in my spirit of this working, but my body still recalled the trauma I'd gone through. I held onto this impossible thing being done through the invisible work of God, knowing He had to be doing something.

Somehow, minute after minute went by, and nothing changed. Carston was perfectly fine, no retracting or working hard to breathe, all vitals were normal, and he was actually getting sleepy, almost ready for bed. We went ahead and changed his diaper, lead stickers, and his clothes. I will never forget his nurse asking me to hold the tube of oxygen by his nose so we could take off his mask to clean his mouth and eyes. I thought for sure that having no pressure in his lungs at all could ruin everything, but it was something we had to do, check his skin for any irritation and make adjustments to his mask. It actually turned out fine. He loved the quick break, but the poor guy was startled when the nurse put it back on his nose.

He was worn out by the time we were finished with his entire care, so I swaddled him up tight and laid him on his side, which he loved. When he was intubated, he could not lay comfortably on his side due to the neo bar always being in the way, pushing his cheek over. I patted Carston's back and rubbed his head until he fell asleep. None of us could believe our eyes, not me, not my nurse, or any of the doctors—he was doing it, he was breathing, he really was!

Miracle #12

Carston breathed on his own, free from the ventilator.

"Through faith in the name of Jesus this man was healed
—and you know how crippled he was before.
Faith in Jesus' Name has healed him
before your very eyes."

ACTS 3:16, NLT

Monday, November 21, 2016

It's been four days now, and Carston is still on CiPAP! Every sleep-less night and stressful day is worth it, as we see Carston's purpose unfold right before our eyes. He's been doing so well that yesterday doctors lowered his oxygen and pressure settings! HALLELUJAH! GOD is literally working right before us! Doctors were thinking death, but I've always believed in healing and perfect LIFE! This is REDEMPTION season! God is fighting this battle and renewing Carston from the top of his head *to the soles of his feet. This morning we took his mask off for about five minutes to wash his face and head, and he was breathing on his own the whole time with no problems!*

Pastor Teague came by today like he does every Monday and brought a little gift with him. As pastor says, Carston keeps throwing the doctors curveballs, so what's more appropriate than this little baseball cap! He's just so adorable in it and happier than ever! My little man is almost three months old and weighs 6 lbs. now, pretty small but gaining weight every day. Our God is so good and always on time! REJOICE, REJOICE, and again I say REJOICE!

It was a long journey to receive this miracle, seventy-five days of testing my faith for deliverance to finally arrive, for Carston to be freed and breathe once again on his own. As I was going through the waiting, fighting this battle, I couldn't help but think why it was taking so long. I received answers and healings for Carston through the beginning of my journey with haste, but now I know, sometimes it takes constant prayer and time with God to gradually release the miracle. In the waiting, God was working. He was crafting this whole messy battle into a much more powerful victory than I could have imagined. It was impossible, then, to see why we had to endure so many failed extubations. But without the long fight, without God eliminating every possible option and medical intervention, His true power would have never been revealed. Every drug had to be tried, every doctor's strategy put to the test. If Carston breathed fine after recovery, he would have been just like any other patient, and God would not have received the glory. It would have resulted in a coincidence or credit to the doctors' wisdom. *Without the battle, there is no miracle.* It was God, and God alone.

The heavens were rejoicing, and everyone I knew on earth couldn't contain their excitement over this victory. I finally had a season of relief and rest to follow, a time to just cradle my son in pure amazement as his momma, not his army. It was a refreshing time of praise to my God, and still to this day, I can't give enough back to Him for keeping His promise and freeing my son.

ARTILLERY VAULT

Keep these verses at the ready for when you need strength in the waiting.

➤——→ LUKE 10:19

➤——→ 2 CORINTHIANS 5:7

➤——→ 2 CORINTHIANS 3:17

➤——→ PSALM 34:4

➤——→ 2 CORINTHIANS 4:8–9

➤——→ DANIEL 10:2–14

➤——→ MATTHEW 19:26

➤——→ ACTS 3:16

➤——→ PROVERS 16:9

FAITH CHECKPOINT

*Search your heart and fortify the walls of your faith to
ensure security through the terrain of the unknown.*

Battle from the Holy Place

In our seasons of what seems like silence from God, it can be easy to come up
with our own method of solving the problem, but we have to be careful with
our solutions because nothing will make us feel more alone than a wrongly
interpreted season. God's silence is not absence; He is always with us even if we
haven't received the answer or blessing we've pressed in for. God has a reason
for waiting to deliver, so trust Him! In some instances, the middle of the chaos
is just louder than God's voice, but I want to encourage you to find a place to
be still and regroup before losing the course God intended for you to travel.

In this waiting time, the Holy Spirit almost always leads me to fast, giving
up part of what may be sustaining my flesh to ultimately rely totally on God in
the physical and spiritual realms. He draws my mind and heart away from the
distractions to intentionally listen for the quiet direction of the Lord.

*"In their hearts humans plan their course,
but the LORD establishes their steps."*

PROVERBS 16:9

What is it that you need revelation for or confidence in today? In my waiting, I often think of Abraham. For twenty-five years, he anticipated God to fulfill His initial promise of making him a great nation, with all families of the earth being blessed through him. He was one hundred, and Sarah was ninety when she finally had Isaac. In their waiting, they certainly tried thinking of how God would give them a family—maybe through Abraham's steward, Eliezer, or Sarah's slave, Hagar? But through their obedience, God created a miracle with Sarah giving birth in her old age (Genesis 12–15.) Now Abraham is commonly known as the Father of Faith; we can look to him knowing that if we remain true to God, He will work all things out in His timing for a greater purpose than we can even imagine. Right now, God is working and has a purpose in the quiet, still moments when we don't understand it. You are a key part of God's strategy for victory in the battle, so rank up in faith and remember,

- Our tiredness, uncertainty, and overwhelmed feeling in battle is not defeat.

- Requesting the impossible requires invisible work from God.

- The messier the battle, the more meaningful the victory.

WEAPONS OF TRUTH

What does Scripture say about the Lord's power
to get us through the waiting?

Look up the following verses in your Bible and write down what they say. Spend a moment thinking about what each verse says about *how we rise up in unpredictable times of suffering,* specifically. How will you respond to these truths today? Write it down.

ISAIAH 30:18

_____

_____

_____

_____

_____

MICAH 7:7

_____

_____

_____

_____

_____

EPHESIANS 3:20–21

_____

_____

_____

_____

_____

PHILIPPIANS 4:7–13

_____

_____

_____

_____

_____

ADDITIONAL NOTES:

_____

_____

_____

_____

_____

_____

_____

CHAPTER 9

Growing in Glory and Grace

*"And my God will meet all your needs
according to the riches of his glory in Christ Jesus.
To our God and Father be glory
for ever and ever.
Amen."*

PHILIPPIANS 4:19–20

WE HAD DONE IT. We defeated Satan! Carston was breathing, and I couldn't help being his biggest, most annoying fan, cheering him on and telling everyone about his progress. I think I was singing praises in my sleep, consumed by how good God was to me. He showed me He was with me through everything, even in His silence, which ranked up my faith as I won the battle with the artillery He provided. Again, I was consumed in the blessings as I surrendered to the power of prayer, wearing the armor of God, using His Scriptures as my sword, giving God thanks and praise in the midst of my darkness, believing without doubt, and fasting. He heard and answered every prayer I offered. It took a lot of faith to put it all out there; all I could do was hope and believe, but having lived through it, I'm a true witness of the victory.

After an astounding week of Carston's breathing improving day by day, they moved him down to CPAP. The doctors made further plans to try a full-time nasal cannula the following week in an effort to get him home in time for Christmas. With Carston being off the ventilator, he was able to make new advances out of nowhere, and we enjoyed him at ease as he grew more independent. Keeping him out of bed with no limit on time was the most freeing experience. If he wasn't in my arms, he cried to be in his baby swing, making it simple for Trinity to reach him. We made countless memories as we watched her be totally hands-on. She helped herself to the nurse's desk, grabbing towels and blankets to cover him up, and she wouldn't settle until she could get her hands on the sponge tip to give him a drink. One time the nurse caught her and asked, "Are you going to be a nurse one day?" But Trinity quickly corrected her, saying, "No, a doctor!" I will never forget that moment, not having a care in the world. We all just laughed.

It took many more days than expected to use the nasal cannula, but Carston's body was finally ready for time away from his mask. He practiced with the nasal cannula and rocked it! Physical therapy also claimed a place in our daily schedule to relax Carston's clenched fists. He didn't like the rolled cotton in his palms, but the therapy allowed his fingers to function and his hands to open up.

Every small advancement was a huge milestone for us, including moving up a size in clothing. Finally, at three months old, it was out with the preemie size and in with the newborn size. His closet was full of cozy, rich styles we just couldn't find before, so we had to celebrate with multiple outfit changes and pictures. I made great efforts to use our handstitched candy cane blanket for the photo backdrop, but Carston cried as soon as I laid him down. So I picked him back up, and, of course, he stopped. I bounced him for a minute, then tried to lay him back down, and nope, he just cried! Every time I think of this, I can't help but smile; he knew it was me, his momma.

Although the majority of our stay in the NICU was serious and heavy, we had our sentimental times right along with the many miracles that outshined the darkness. That's the season we were living in, just bliss. I was excited and had no worries; we were almost home. This happy time lasted almost four weeks. We built on each victory as Carston continued to hit home runs with his breathing, but by mid-December, we made some decisions that changed everything.

"Let us then approach God's throne of grace with confidence,
so that we may receive mercy and find grace to help us in our time of need."

HEBREWS 4:16

Welcome His Wisdom

Everyone was amazed by Carston's progress, so much so, the doctors considered weening some of Carston's medications, starting with Erythromycin. I was elated, thinking the less meds the better, but Carston's body didn't agree; he began spitting up a lot. It didn't help that my milk supply ran low that same week, and they had to use Similac® Organic to supplement the feedings. Carston then began spitting up 20mls at a time. I was shocked to witness him doing that, I think we all were, so the doctors went straight back to using only my frozen milk (well, what was left of it), which helped.

I struggled so hard with this because I was responsible for his milk; I wanted to supply everything he needed, but even with all the help provided, I couldn't reach my milk production goals and felt so guilty. Amber sent me lactation cookies and gave me advice on how to increase my milk supply, along with the tips from the lactation nurse at the hospital. I had all the tools, but nothing was working. I pumped and pumped for almost four months, doing so great I even had to freeze three grocery bags full in the beginning, which made it hard to believe I was already running out and my body was drying up. The lactation nurse said it could have had something to do with the little sleep I was getting and my lack of nutrition and motivation. She tried to make me feel better, but the enemy kept shouting, "Failure!" so loudly in my mind. Carston needed the best, and I was trying, but we still had to push forward with other options.

After two days, Carston's stomach was somewhat settled, and we tried a different formula called Similac® Alimentum®, which was more broken down and easier for him to digest. Although there was an improvement in his feeds, that week of puking and milk changes didn't happen without taking a hit on his breathing. Several x-rays showed air in his belly and abdomen, which pushed up on his diaphragm, causing his lungs to be squished. The nasal cannula grew to be a further and further reach as the doctors gradually went up on his oxygen and pressure through CPAP to keep his lungs open. After a steady day on this new formula, his oxygen given through the ventilator was 29%, which thankfully lowered from 45% the day prior.

Carston was so good at throwing these curveballs. The doctors had to take it slow and not push to lower his settings much more, giving his lungs a chance to gain "respiratory reserve," they said. I knew that was best for him but wanted him to breathe freely right then. I wanted my baby out of there and home for Christmas. It was so hard to accept that after my sheer obedience to God, that wasn't going to happen. I knew getting him home wasn't part of the confirmation God had given me. I only asked that Carston would breathe on his own, and God had already blessed me with that, but why not further send him to live a full life with his family?

I wanted to keep loving on Carston so bad, just love him, but it turns out this mission had me more of a fighter. I couldn't understand why the season of triumph was leaving so abruptly, and there I was battling the enemy again. I fought for miracles, I fought for healings, I fought for peace, and I fought for God's will for Carston, and now I had to fight for my own sense of security. I knew it was God's will to heal, but how would the healing happen with my son? It was like the beginning all over again, and I wasn't expecting more battles. I was more mad than broken, angry that God was allowing this to happen. I cried out many times, "Where are you?" and "What more do you want me to do, God?"

Days of anger allowed the enemy to blind me with only disappointments and a lack of hope. I wasn't productive and couldn't function. What was the point? I didn't want to feel that way, but it was easier, that is until

I realized how much I had lost. I had given up good time with Carston to wallow. How pathetic I felt. Even with the misfortune of my milk slowing, I knew God was still good. With the help of CPAP, Carston was breathing on his own, and as I'd witnessed in the past, I had to trust God's plan. I ran to God, relinquishing control in surrender once again, knowing the enemy would flee from me (James 4:7). All selfishness aside, I had to replant my feet on the rock, not the things I was seeing and emotionally distracted by. God was the Rock, and through all my doubt, I didn't deserve His grace, but He was always there in my waiting, wondering, and wallowing. The more I prayed as each day passed, I could feel God so strongly say, "It's all for a purpose." I asked for God's wisdom and easily found through His grace that it's not about ending the battle but recognizing He was in it with me.

On Christmas Eve, Justin and I had a big day in store for Carston. It was so important this day went well because the week leading up to Christmas, I was sick and couldn't make it in to see him. I missed him so much during my time away but prayed eagerly for God's glory to just fall on him. I so desperately wanted things to get better.

On my way to the hospital, I couldn't resist the urge to buy a Christmas tree for his room. I ran across a skinny gold tree that stood as tall as me, and I also grabbed a couple of ornaments in the gift shop at the hospital on my way up to the NICU floor. One ornament was a little boy with a cape that declared "Hero" on his chest, and the other was a large silver ornament that reads "Hope." No doubt they were created just for Carston.

Early morning rounds couldn't have gone better. To my surprise, when I was away, Carston's attending physician had changed. The hospital rotates these doctors about every two months, but I never really had one I connected with until then. She spoke very calmly and gently, and I was shocked that she took an immediate interest, in my opinion, moving forward and thoughts of everything that had happened so far. She went on to tell me that Carston was still on Similac® Alimentum® and had only had a couple of small spit-ups in the last four days. I couldn't stop praising God. This was a much-needed prayer answered over the one thing holding Carston back from breathing. I was so ready to move forward! Until this point, there wasn't a single doctor the enemy didn't have his way with, planting doubt to combat me for reasoning and answers to move forward. So despite setbacks from the previous weeks, feeling a sense of hope from this doctor was something new, and I was confident God wouldn't lead me astray.

Carston was still on a CPAP pressure of 8 and 32% oxygen, but she was hoping to get it down to 27% and his pressure down to a 6 as soon as possible. A 4 is where he needed to be to use the nasal cannula. I was glad to hear her making goals for Carston and believing he could get there.

We continued our day with lots of cuddles and some tummy time on his Boppy® pillow. Once he woke up from his nap, I changed his clothes for another attempt at a Christmas picture, which actually worked out that time. He wore a green bib that read "Santa's Elf!" and loved breathing without his mask. I never took time with Carston for granted, but taking festive photos and putting up a tree in the NICU were not at all part of how I pictured Christmas. I had peace that he was where God wanted him, but creating Christmas joy when it should have been naturally abundant made it hard to be certain of what we were doing there. What was the point of Carston still being in the hospital?

The same underlying sadness from the days leading up to Christmas gripped me as we needed to spend our day away from Carston. I wanted to be with him, but Trinity was so excited for this day, and I couldn't let her down again. I often felt as though I wasn't enough for one of my children, but I was so humbled that on Christmas day, Laila was the one who snuggled and rocked him when we were gone. She even called me to let us know Carston hit seven pounds which made me smile. God blessed me in the little things; He was taking care of my heart along with my son.

With this progress, the Monday after Christmas, doctors made adjustments to Carston's feed time in hopes to still get him home soon. His milk usually got pushed into his belly over a ninety-minute timeframe, but they crunched it down to sixty minutes, which he hated, and his body rejected. Carston was puking up milk after every feed, causing his breathing to suffer again. Witnessing this, I could no longer hold back my tears. I was frustrated and saddened for him, as no child should be getting sick every time they eat. The doctors thought he was aspirating milk into his lungs, so after a day, they changed the feed time back to ninety minutes. He still puked a little bit after every feed for the next two days, but finally, it stopped. His doctor literally said if he puked one more time, we would stop his formula and go back to IV nutrition.

Though it didn't appear we were moving forward, I held onto the fact that Carston was stable, and we continued to figure him out. My patience was being tested. The only thing I knew was that the hospital was to be Carston's home for that period of time, but I surely thought God didn't mean forever. Not knowing what exactly God had planned next, I still lifted up the desires of my heart and continued to believe things would get better.

———

Sunday, January 1, 2017

It's a new year for Carston! A year to be filled with new victories, new milestones, and new strength. I don't care about what happened yesterday or three weeks ago; I claim that this year is a fresh awakening for us all—for Carston, for Justin, and for me. We need a stirring and new joy. We need to see increased progress, miraculous healings, and continuous moves of the Spirit, and I know God is able to do it! When things don't make sense and are complicated, we will press on. I can't calculate God's plans; all I know is that He is a God of completion, and He will either heal Carston on Earth or make him totally complete in Heaven, but I refuse to end his life out of doubt that things can't get better.

It all brings us to this point: there is nothing the doctors can help do to get him off CPAP or help him with his digestion, so we are just waiting on Carston's body to do the work now, or in my opinion, for God to re-create what is broken, the miracle work He has done before, and I know He will do again! Thank you, Lord, for your mighty power and hand in our situation. This year we are ready! This year we WILL see more great things happen! We proclaim these things in Jesus' Name!

#prayersforcarston

———

"If your child asks for bread, do you trick him with sawdust?
If he asks for fish, do you scare him with a live snake on his plate?
As bad as you are, you wouldn't think of such a thing.
You're at least decent to your own children.
So don't you think the God who conceived you in love
will be even better?"

MATTHEW 7:9–11 MSG

I knew without a doubt God wanted me to keep believing that through Him, anything is possible, through Him and His ways. But it didn't come without the pain of giving up everything to God's power, again and again, every day. God's power was giant compared to my control, so I had to turn to Him and repent, being careful not to throw out His power in favor of my own. Deeper and deeper into surrender I became, my persistent enthusiasm slipped away, and silence filled this season. Specific words in my prayers just crumbled; I had no personal desires, no special requests I could utter. His better was greater than my better for Carston. I could sense things were shifting spiritually; I wanted God to prove Himself, to once and for all set Carston free, and I had no choice but to completely leave it in His hands to do it.

ARTILLERY VAULT

*Keep these verses at the ready for when you need God's
grace to get you through uncertainty and heartache.*

≫——▸ PHILIPPIANS 4:19–20

≫——▹ HEBREWS 4:16

▭——▹ JAMES 4:7

▭——▸ MATTHEW 7:9–11

≫——▸ 2 CORINTHIANS 12:9

≫——▹ 1 PETER 1:6–7

≫——▹ JAMES 1:2–4

≫——▹ 2 CORINTHIANS 3:18

FAITH CHECKPOINT

*Search your heart and fortify the walls of your faith to
ensure security through the terrain of the unknown.*

Growing through Grace, Giving Him Glory

Immerse yourself in God's grace, His favor towards you, that He's working on a purpose for your entire struggle and will sustain you through it all.
Sometimes our trials seem to be more than we can bear on our own, and
God allows this so that we give up our own power and give in to His. "My
grace is sufficient for you, for my power is made perfect in weakness," He
says in 2 Corinthians 12:9. Through our not enough and our mistakes, God's
grace fills us with what we need to carry on, even when we don't deserve it.
No matter what mountain you're climbing or dark valley you are walking in,
continue to trust God on a greater level, where you don't have to know the
details of His plan to know He will bring victory.

To stay hopeful when nothing makes sense, remember that God will
bring purpose to the pain you may be experiencing. Peter tells us in 1 Peter
1:6–7 that trials produce genuineness of your faith, and James encourages
us in James 1:2–4 to consider trials joy because they produce perseverance
within you, making you complete and lacking nothing. Paul explains in 2
Corinthians 3:18 that you are being transformed from one degree of glory to
another. Obedience and surrender to God are key parts in the ability to carry
on giving Him glory through the toughest parts of your battle. When you
can't see the physical manifestations of your faith right here and now, know
God is working to better your life for whatever is coming next. Rank up in
faith and remember:

- In asking for God's wisdom, we can easily find through His
  grace that it's not about ending the battle but recognizing
  He's in it with us.

- God's power is giant compared to our control, so turn to Him
  and refuse to throw out His power in favor of your own.

- Rejoice in the expectation of God's glory being fulfilled, not in how we expect our blessing to unfold.

WEAPONS OF TRUTH

What does Scripture say about God's grace and His purpose for our trials?

Look up the following verses in your Bible and write down what they say. Spend a moment thinking about what each verse says about *how we should respond to our trials and the purpose God has for them*, specifically. How will you respond to these truths today? Write it down.

Isaiah 30:18

_____

_____

_____

_____

_____

ACTS 20:24

_____

_____

_____

_____

_____

2 CORINTHIANS 12:9

_____

_____

_____

_____

_____

1 PETER 4:13

_____

_____

_____

_____

_____

ADDITIONAL NOTES:

_____

_____

_____

CHAPTER 10

Peace in His Courts

"Lord God All-Powerful, the God of Jacob, please answer my prayer!
You are the shield that protects your people, and I am your chosen one.
Won't you smile on me? One day in your temple is better than a thousand anywhere
else. I would rather serve in your house, than live in the homes of the wicked.
Our Lord and our God, you are like the sun and also like a shield.
You treat us with kindness and with honor, never denying any good thing to those
who live right. Lord God All-Powerful, you bless everyone who trusts you."

PSALM 84:8–12 CEV

A WEEK INTO THE NEW YEAR, NOTHING HAD GOTTEN BETTER; NOTH-ING GREAT HAD HAPPENED; IN FACT, THINGS GOT MUCH WORSE. Four months with Carston, and still, there wasn't a day I could predict. Would there be progress, or did God have other plans? One evening I called in to check on Carston before I went to bed, and all of my expectations for him began to unravel.

The nightshift nurse reported him being a little fussy with his evening care, so she bumped his oxygen up to get him through it. He was at 40% through the mask, but 28% was his normal, so although she assured me he was doing fine, it still concerned me. Sure enough, I got a startling call from the NNP at 2:30 a.m. saying he went from needing 40% all the way up to 100% oxygen. Something was really wrong. 100% oxygen given through CPAP should have been enough to keep the oxygen saturation in his lungs above 85%, but it only read 70%. She said they were doing everything they could to keep him from being intubated, and at that moment, I knew I had to get to the hospital as fast as possible.

Once I arrived, the NNP met me in the hallway and explained how uncomfortable and irritated Carston was, thrashing around, waving his arms a lot, sticking his tongue in and out as if he was refluxing, head bobbing, and tugging due to the struggle to breathe. As we walked toward his room, she continued on saying how his nurse tried many ways to calm him—his swing, Boppy® pillow, patting and holding him, nothing would ease him longer than about twenty minutes. They gave him two doses of Tylenol® and Ativan® in hopes of relaxing him, but those wore off quickly, and nothing seemed to help. As a last resort, they had to intubate him due to his heart rate also dropping into the 60s.

I sped ahead of her into my son's room, rushing away from everything she said, but turmoil hit me when I saw the tube down his throat. What she said was reality, and I almost collapsed right there on the floor. Knowing God had a plan got me through each difficult moment in the past, but this time it just brought more pain. I wasn't hearing from God, and He still wasn't bringing the miraculous things I knew He could. I wondered if this was part of His design? Was I meant to feel and accept that this could be the end? I was never guaranteed how much time Carston had with us, was I supposed to keep fighting? New questions and doubts that I'd never let in began to fill my mind. My baby was again struggling to do the simplest thing for every human being, to just breathe. I was hurting and exhausted on the inside, trying my best not to let this consume me. The doctors' suggestion to end things always sat heavily in my mind unless I actively worked to dismiss it, but in these moments, it was so hard to fight back.

Initially, we didn't know what made Carston's body so weak, but the doctors still did everything they could to find answers. Before they intubated Carston, they took an x-ray of his lungs, checked for feeding tube placement, and took a blood gas; all of these things came back normal. Carston also received a heart echo and EKG, which revealed his heart was the same as it was a couple of months ago, but cardiology noticed the right side of Carston's heart growing larger than normal. It was overworking to regulate the oxygen pressure in his lungs, so the harder it pumped, the larger it became, which would have led to heart failure. To try and prevent that from moving forward, we had to make sure Carston's oxygen saturation stayed above 90% instead of 85%. If the oxygen in his lungs got below 90%, we had to turn up the oxygen on his ventilator. His vent was already giving him 65% after everything that happened that night, and although this would solve one problem, the cardiologists predicted it would cause another by making his heart pump extra blood to his lungs. The band surgery could help this, but Carston was not stable enough for a procedure like that, which again left me with no options but to give into whatever God had next, believing it was a re-creation of his heart.

As if his trouble breathing wasn't enough, Carston's feeds were continuously dripping into his tummy. After his struggle to breathe, they stopped his food that was given in a ninety-minute time frame. When they intubated and started his food again, he couldn't handle it within the ninety minutes, which was the time needed for him to get back to CPAP. He just spit up his milk everywhere. How many times can a mother's heart break? I wanted good things for my son, but instead, he felt sick, and I felt sick. I wanted him to enjoy his life, not feel miserable in it, but we were so far from that, it seemed.

That day, I heard words being said about Carston like "needing to cooperate," "acting up," and other comments of the same. It didn't make things any better. This wasn't my son's fault. My boy was a good, sweet, sweet boy, just fighting a terrible condition. I could see it, though, in the doctors and nurses. They were all just so tired, and like me, they didn't know why or what was next to come. Our hearts were troubled for what he had to endure. I was barely hanging on to my faith at this point. I knew of my weapons, I knew strategy, but I was so weak and needed help; I desperately begged God for answers and direction. I asked everyone to pray for three specific needs and healings over Carston:

1. Carston's heart and lungs would improve communication between one another to hopefully prevent surgery as long as possible.

2. We could bring Carston's oxygen down under 30% (preferably to 21%) on his machine, with less mucus coming from his lungs.

3. Carston's belly would allow the transition back to ninety-minute feeds without any spit-ups.

I felt like things had to supernaturally get better once more, as there was nothing the doctors could do, so it was time for God's ultimate plan to be revealed. After ten days of staying overnight at the hospital again, I wasn't sure how much more I could take. All night, every night, the physical chaos around me just wouldn't stop. I would jump at every beeping notification in Carston's room, awakened by random alarms going off in the hallway, bright lights, doctors and nurses in and out, wondering what they were up to. Trying to keep myself updated, rested, positive, and alert was impossible. I was my son's advocate, his voice, and his fighter, but I wasn't sure how much longer I could fight. Carston was actually getting worse. His oxygen intake on the ventilator was still 65%, and he had a lot of mucus coming out of his lungs, so things weren't looking promising. Up until that point, I had been so confident and could make important decisions, but my mind became clouded and my spirit unsure of how to proceed. I always believed in God's power and ability, and nothing would stop that, but I was still seeking clarity on the reason for all this. I wondered if I was selfish for pushing him through these challenges. How long was God's plan meant to take for healing, all year? Or even years, maybe lifelong for Carston? Overthinking surely distorted my spiritual sense of what God was saying was supposed to be next. I had to let go of any effort of my own to move forward and wait on God to do something or reveal something to me, whatever His will was.

"Then Jesus said, 'Did I not tell you that if you believe, you will see the glory of God?' So they took away the stone. Then Jesus looked up and said, 'Father, I thank you that you have heard me. I knew that you always hear me, but I said this for the benefit of the people standing here, that they may believe that you sent me.' When he had said this, Jesus called in a loud voice, 'Lazarus, come out!' The dead man came out, his hands and feet wrapped with strips of linen, and a cloth around his face. Jesus said to them, 'Take off the grave clothes and let him go.'"

JOHN 11:40–44

Release and Believe

Another week went by, and I remained very impatient in my waiting. One morning when I was holding Carston, out of nowhere, his heart rate dropped into the 50s and oxygen into the 30s. Alarms went off with the same frantic routine. Doctors and nurses rushed in from everywhere, surrounding us and moving him back into his bed, first checking his breathing tube placement to be sure it hadn't come out, which it hadn't, then analyzing the rest of his body and the machines. It was scary watching his numbers go down further and further, knowing I had the most intelligent, experienced doctors by his side. They were bagging him, forcing breaths into his lungs at a steady pace for about five minutes. They tried Ativan® to help calm him, but nothing was helping him come out of this. I was praying for God to help him, and as they were working, eventually, everything started creeping back up to his normal.

The doctors explained to me something I never heard before, that Carston went through a first-degree heart block, where the blood wasn't being pushed through his vessels properly, causing the collapse. They weren't sure if this would be a reoccurring thing, so we kept a close eye on him throughout the day, and thankfully, nothing else out of the ordinary happened. At this point, I needed to go home. I felt like I could collapse, but I wanted a family member with him through the night, so around 9:00 p.m., my mom came and took my place.

At 2:00 a.m. that morning, I was awakened by a phone call from my mom, who was hysterical, crying, "Carston is in another heart block!" His heart rate and oxygen saturation weren't as low as earlier in the day, and his first heart block lasted only five minutes, so I stayed on the phone and prayed he would come right out of it, and after about twenty minutes, he did. With no energy or adrenaline left within me, I had to get sleep and planned to head up early the next morning. It's unbelievable how out of it I was. I was more than exhausted; I truly had nothing left to offer.

At 7:00 a.m., Justin and I were driving to the hospital when we got a call from my mom, but she couldn't speak. The doctor took the phone and told us Carston was in another heart block, this time more severe. His oxygen was in the teens and heart rate at 30. They felt like he was passing and wanted to prepare me that he might pass before I got there.

Immediately, I was in a disarray of emotions. Any time death was mentioned before, I could laugh in the devil's face, but at this point, I couldn't form any gestures or words. I wondered how much more I could fight, could

Carston fight? I knew I couldn't bear this heartache much longer. I ultimately wanted God's will to be done, His greatness for Carston here on Earth, but for the first time, there was a shift in my spirit, and out of a new surrender, I cried, "Lord, if You want Carston, I free him to You."

I would have never professed something like that through our whole battle, but I could sense the Holy Spirit confirming that I was in the right place. Carston had been through so much and always pulled through on top. And no matter what was to happen next, we still won because God always wins. I prayed the whole way to the hospital that if God was going to take him, He would allow me to be with him, hold him, and say our goodbyes, but somehow in the same breath, I still believed God could do anything.

Pastor Teague got our whole church praying, and by the time we arrived at the hospital, Carston was already out of heart block. All his numbers looked close to normal, and the doctors were stunned! Due to things getting so bad, they gave Carston morphine to help him relax, which suppresses the lungs, yet his lungs got better. Our pastor and intercessors showed up to pray over Carston later in the day, which really blessed us. Someone in the room mentioned how God raised Lazarus from the dead and can do anything for Carston as well. Even after Carston would take his last breath, God could still re-create what's broken within him; it's never too late.

I never let go of God's power to do whatever He chooses, but later that night, Carston was again in and out of heart blocks until 6:15 a.m. the next morning. I was so sorry that he was going through this but followed God's lead, knowing I'd done all I could do; I drained every ounce of myself into the battle. I lifted up all my prayers, begged, pleaded, and stood unwavering right beside my God through many victories. I praised and rejoiced one day, only to be shoved in a valley the next, over and over again. I felt so alone in this world even though God was still nearby. I felt like no one understood what I was going through, and no one could actually rescue me from the pain I felt for my son and from this long battle.

At 6:15 a.m., things got scary. The room was loud with doctors flying in from everywhere when all of a sudden, Carston's heart stopped. Nothing happened for over a minute, no breathing, and no heart function. My whole world shut down, all the chaos spinning around me from day one stopped. Within the silence, my heart also sank into the deepest part of my chest. Everyone thought he was gone, the alarms were silenced, and his room was still; you couldn't hear a single breath from the many doctors surrounding us.

Carston was given no compressions or medications to bring him back, a hard decision made days ago when these heart blocks started. Doctors warned us that these interventions would not help his heart with the irregular rhythm, and compressions would break ribs and cause more complications. So in total shock, I sat still, a hush was over the room, and all I could do as an instinct was pray, "Jesus help him."

The nurses were watching the clock, and every second drug out as I was holding onto this precious life, this life with no heartbeat, this life with no breath. The clock hit ninety seconds, and somehow his heart randomly started beating again, and everything came right back up to his normal baseline. Carston was back, re-created and renewed!

Miracle #13

Carston came back to life after ninety seconds without a heartbeat. Revived from death.

"'Though the mountains be shaken and the hills be removed,
yet my unfailing love for you not be shaken
nor my covenant of peace be removed,' says the LORD,
who has compassion for you."

ISAIAH 54:10

Saturday, January 21, 2017

It's been unbelievable weening Carston's settings for the past six days. All I've really needed is quality time with him, without worry, and God is good—He is giving me that. There is no mucus coming from his lungs now, and each day is just getting better and better. There hasn't been a single visit from a doctor, nurse, physical therapist, or chaplain where they haven't entered with a huge smile, not knowing where to begin.

Carston is bringing new joy and hope to the NICU, revealing what only God can do, what I have been talking about from the beginning. The strength of my faith initially gave me a lot of crazy looks, convincing doctors I'm naïve and simply uneducated, but we are conquering every diagnosis and even death in more ways than just one, reaching the doubters and unbelievers, and that's all I could ask for.

I'm a stubborn girl, and it took God to bring me to the end of myself, time and time again, for me to realize that if I just let go of all of me and believe in all of Him, it will get me the victory. When I am weak, He is strong. He goes before me in battle. He fights for me because I am His child. Sometimes, as children, we can't fully comprehend how our guardian protects us, and how they plan what's best for us, making it hard always to accept the outcome. For me, this wasn't the end of the struggle, but it wasn't the final victory either. Ahead was a whole new journey of accepting God's will, finding answers in His presence and words.

ARTILLERY VAULT

Keep these verses at the ready for when you are tired
and need the Lord's clarity and refueling.

➤———→ PSALM 84:8–12

➤———→ JOHN 11:40–44

➤———→ ISAIAH 54:10

➤———→ ISAIAH 40:31

FAITH CHECKPOINT

Search your heart and fortify the walls of your faith to
ensure security through the terrain of the unknown.

Reunited into Peace

Isaiah 40:31 says that if we wait on the Lord, we gain new strength, so how can He overcome our exhaustion if we refuse to lay down in His arms? Our brains and bodies are wired to go, to mentally prepare, emotionally process, and physically achieve, however at some point, the body has to give way to the Lord's ultimate design. We can't carry our emotions and physical pain on our own. Releasing the grip completely from our plans, requests, and actions, no matter how holy our efforts are, will bring healing and a new focus on what God desires for our lives.

Are you stuck in a place where you are tired and hurting? A place where it's difficult to understand the point of the good things in the past and have hope that peace can come out of it in the future? Hold close the story of our savior; Jesus was beaten and physically destroyed on the cross, yet new life was brought forth through the breaking. Death did not win, for everlasting life prevailed! Jesus endured suffering for the greatest reward of all time. I encourage you to persevere in your desperate situation, knowing that the breaking you experience may be part of your personal testimony but is a small component of a greater purpose you are assigned. Rank up in faith and remember,

- Overthinking can distort our spiritual sense of what God is saying is supposed to be next.

- Sometimes, as children, we can't fully comprehend how our Heavenly Guardian protects us, how He plans what is best for us.

- No matter what is to happen at the end of your battle, you still win because God is fighting for you, and He always wins.

WEAPONS OF TRUTH

*What does Scripture say about God's peace
and rest amidst our suffering?*

Look up the following verses in your Bible and write down what they say.
Spend a moment thinking about what each verse says about *obtaining peace
when things around us don't make sense.* How will you respond to these truths
today? Write it down.

JOB 22:21–22

_____

_____

_____

_____

_____

PSALM 27:13–14

_____

_____

_____

_____

_____

PSALM 37:7

_____

_____

_____

_____

_____

MATTHEW 11:28–30

_____

_____

_____

_____

ADDITIONAL NOTES:

_____

_____

_____

_____

_____

_____

_____

CHAPTER II

On the Seventh Day, We Rest

*"The righteous cry out, and the LORD hears them; he delivers them
from all their troubles. The LORD is close to the brokenhearted
and saves those who are crushed in spirit. The righteous person may
have many troubles, but the LORD delivers him from them all;
he protects all his bones, not one of them will be broken."*

PSALM 34:17–20

IT WAS JANUARY 29, THE DAY BEFORE TRINITY'S BIRTHDAY, WHEN A CALL CAME IN FROM THE HOSPITAL AT 4:30 A.M. CARSTON WAS IN HEART BLOCK AGAIN OUT OF NOWHERE. I got up and going, holding my composure and center of peace, knowing I had no physical way to change the situation. I stayed in submission, trusting in God and letting Him know that.

I arrived around 5:30 a.m. and held Carston for two hours, but he didn't improve at all like I was sure he would, so I decided to call Justin. I told him that Carston was still in heart block; it was the longest he'd ever had, and I needed him to come to be there with us.

At 9:00 a.m., Justin and Trinity pulled into the hospital. Carston was still in heart block. Concerned about what could happen next, his doctor came to discuss giving him an IV. During that conversation, his heart rate and oxygen dropped right from 50 down to zero in a matter of minutes. Carston's monitors should have been beeping like crazy, which would have sent the whole NICU a Code Blue to Carston's room, but this time things were different. All alarms were muted, and no one rushed in to help. The room was still, but my mind was spinning, and with a huge lump in my throat, I insisted the NNP give him every med possible to bring him back, going against my initial requests.

Tears filled my eyes, and out of nowhere, a wave of peace flushed over me. I couldn't form any thoughts or words, and strangely enough, it didn't feel natural to beg God for another miracle. God had given me quality time with Carston and his improvements that past week so I could truly enjoy him before this moment right here. I sensed it as he lay in my arms. I comforted Carston so tightly, knowing he had left to be with his Creator. He went to rest, and that day, somehow, we rested too.

Thursday, February 9, 2017

Ten days without Carston, and I'm really missing him. In a constant state of tears, I have to get through each day by reminding myself that he's living his best life with Jesus. I cling tight to a word someone shared with me at the showing, that we live here on the Earth where the devil has the opportunity to rob us, but with Carston, he still did not win. God saved him from the endless battle, standing up from the throne and accepting him in at Heaven's gates. The enemy can only take so much; he does have a limit, which is when God steps in with eternal, beautiful, pain-free life.

After all my praying, God did heal him, time and time again, and maybe there would have been more to Carston's life; maybe if I had more to give, he could have kept fighting, but there was nothing left for me to pour out. I have to remember that. I truly did all I could. I came to the point of needing instant peace, and Carston needed peace, so God granted us that. He rescued us from more battle, and so in my wondering, my wrestling, and waking of each day, I still thank the Lord. I know that God knows best, and He cares for my hurting heart.

He's taking care of us now, giving Justin visions of Carston running free in a huge field of tall grass and flowers, healed, waiting for us to all be together one day again. I can't wait to run to him and scoop him up in my arms, holding him tight and laughing with joy. At that moment, he will never leave my sight again.

God couldn't have chosen a more improbable candidate to prove He still heals than for a headstrong mother to show the world you can still have faith through an unpredictable outcome. One thing I do know is that through it all, our God is still good. He always provides and performs on time in ways better than we could on our own. I will continue to trust Him no matter what my future holds, even through trial and tribulation, because He knows me and the course of my life better than anyone else.

Throughout my pregnancy and our time in the hospital, there wasn't a day when the enemy didn't come to steal, kill, and destroy. That's what he does; he tried tempting me day in and day out to just end my son's life. Whether it was a medical statistic, an opinion from a nurse, doctor, or counselor, or just the enemy playing scenarios in my mind of how terrible his life would be, the devil constantly tried to find a way in. Yet, God is faithful; He wouldn't let me be tempted beyond what I could bear; in my heart and mind, ending his life was sin against God, but God provided a way out way out so I could endure it, just as it explains in 1 Corinthians 10:13. When I could hardly take much more of the devil's schemes, upon the prompting in my spirit, I released Carston to the Lord to save us from what seemed like hell some days. I didn't know what God would do, but I trusted Him, and so the only thing to believe is that taking Carston was our way out, our way to victory.

Processing it all, Carston was never created to live an ordinary life; no, I had asked God to be used for His Kingdom, so He gave me my son. God chose this assignment for me, a journey much bigger than I would have ever chosen for myself. God gave Carston what life He did to prove He still heals and performs miracles. Carston's whole point in being was to give me mine, his life as a platform to expand the Kingdom of God, living on as a true story to share God's goodness and bring glory to the Father. Whether it's those who were live witnesses, by word of mouth or reading this book, you are all a part of the reason for my son's life. I pray this is your anchor to go deeper with God, praying bigger prayers and believing in the impossible, because with God, all things are possible—He's just waiting to show you.

"While we are alive, we are constantly being handed over to death for Jesus' sake, so that the life of Jesus may be clearly shown in our mortal bodies. And so death is at work in us, but life is at work in you."

2 CORINTHIANS 4:11–12 ISV

13 Works of the Re-Creator

1. God sealed my membranes at 27 weeks. Amniotic fluid increased from 4 cm to 11 cm!

2. God crafted the missing cerebellum and tissue in Carston's brain.

3. Carston flipped from head up to head down into the birthing position on the day I was admitted.

4. The fourth chamber of Carston's heart grew to normal size instead of shrinking as predicted.

5. Carston survived birth.

6. Carston breathed on his own without intubation.

7. Carston made it through stomach and esophagus surgery successfully! His esophageal atresia and hole in his stomach was repaired.

8. Carston's thyroid started working properly, and his heart healed with no sign of SVT.

9. Carston's esophagus was healed! Passed esophagram within four weeks.

10. Carston defeated death as God healed his staph infection.

11. Carston's liver was fully functional. Bilirubin at 16 down to a 1.

12. Carston breathed on his own, free from the ventilator.

13. Carston came back to life after ninety seconds without a heartbeat. Revived from death.

Our trials and suffering can actually bring life to others, and I hope mine did that for you. I want you to know, from the beginning of our mistakes, God could have turned His head in rejection, but His agape love for us brought Him to sacrifice His son's own life. Christ saved us from eternity in hell! We are unworthy, yet He still wants us for eternity. He longs to consume our lives and purify our souls. Every human on this Earth will fail us, but God says in Hebrews 13:5, "Never will I leave you; never will I forsake you." He longs to develop unbreakable relationships with us that contain treasures in hidden places on Earth and in Heaven. This is the beginning of life with no end!

To experience this depth in faith on your own, you can take the first steps of confession and belief by following the instruction of Romans 10:9–10. It is my utmost hope that you would find your purpose through Christ as His child, His soldier, carrying out the very special assignment He has only for you.

"If you declare with your mouth
'Jesus is Lord,'
and believe in your heart
that God raised him from the dead,
you will be saved.
For it is with your heart you believe
and are justified,
and it is with your mouth
that you profess your faith
and are saved."

ROMANS 10:9–10

1. Recognize your sin and ask for God's forgiveness. "If we confess our sins, he is faithful and just and will forgive us our sins and purify us from all unrighteousness." (1 John 1:9)

2. Give control of your life to the Lord. "For whoever wants to save their life will lose it, but whoever loses their life for me and for the gospel will save it." (Mark 8:35)

3. Speak out that you believe Jesus is the son of God who died for your sins, then on the third day rose from the grave to give you eternal life. "This is love: not that we loved God, but that He loved us and sent his Son as an atoning sacrifice for our sins." (1 John 4:10)

4. Believe His word is true and ask Him to come into your heart to be your Lord and Savior. "I have been crucified with Christ and I no longer live, but Christ lives in me. The life I now live in the body, I live by faith in the Son of God, who loved me and gave himself for me." (Galatians 2:20)

Welcome to the Kingdom of God! We're all cheering for you! Even Heaven is rejoicing and will be witnessing your faith journey until the end. Accepting that Jesus Christ took your sin on the cross means you are no longer in bondage to shame. God instantly re-created *your* heart into newness and washed you white as snow. Now it's time to rank up in faith. With confidence, live out this new life! Worship the Lord through song and praise, read God's Word every day, and finally, grab a friend and tell them about your God who does miraculous things!

NOTES

1. Trisomy 18 Foundation, "What is Trisomy 18?";
    https://www.trisomy18.org/what-is-trisomy-18/

2. Rapha: Strong's Concordance #7495; Brown-Driver-Briggs
    Hebrew Lexicon; https://www.bibletools.org/index.cfm/
    fuseaction/Lexicon.show/ID/H7495/rapha.htm

ABOUT THE AUTHOR

Ashley Adams is an inspirational writer, who actively journals God's voice and direction He has for her every day. *Re-Created for Faith* is the birthplace of her ministry. She blindly trusts in God for the next big steps to expand the Kingdom, faithfully using her social media platforms to encourage people through real-life heartache and God's plan for it. Ashley lives to see souls saved, serving as a board member and director at Scioto Youth Camp: Reaching Kids for Christ, along with hosting Bible studies in her home for women of the community.

Ashely and her husband, Justin, now have four children, including their newest baby boy. They recently made a big move out of town and into the country. They now reside on what used to be her great-grandfather's farm of over one hundred acres and are building a new home, excited for what the future holds. Ashley is determined to obey the Lord as He guides, raising tiny disciples through her homeschooling and pressing in on aspirations to adopt more children.

Ashley's faith has been tried by fire, yet she experiences God's blessings ten-fold. To read original posts from Carston's battle, search #prayersforcarston on Facebook. For current updates and encouragement through life, follow Ashley on Facebook and Instagram @ashleyadams4faith.

CPSIA information can be obtained
at www.ICGtesting.com
Printed in the USA
LVHW091540211121
704025LV00020B/771/J